REHOBOTH
A PLACE FOR US

AN ALBUM OF FAMILY STORIES

JAMES C. SCHAAP

FAITH
ALIVE®
Christian Resources

Grand Rapids, Michigan

Printed in the United States of America.

Library of Congress Cataloging-in-Publication Data

Schaap, James C., 1948-
Rehoboth, a place for us : an album of family stories / by James C. Schaap.
    p. cm.
ISBN 978-1-59255-545-1
1. Rehoboth Christian School (Rehoboth, N.M.)—History. 2. Indians of North America—Education—New Mexico—Rehoboth—History. 3. Indian students—New Mexico—Rehoboth—Biography. 4. Christian education—New Mexico—Rehoboth—History. I. Title.
E97.6.R44S34 2010
371.829'97078983—dc22
    2010034494

Front and back cover photos: John Van't Land

Exact Navajo language provided by Irvinson Jones.

10 9 8 7 6 5 4 3 2 1

CONTENTS

A WORD OF THANKS

Years ago I wrote a book for the Christian Reformed Church called *CRC Family Portrait,* a series of stories featuring ordinary members of the denomination. When I was working on that book, Rev. Rolf Veenstra, something of a local legend in and around Rehoboth, told me something I've never forgotten. In no uncertain terms, he said that if I wanted to write a story that featured a Native American in the Rehoboth neighborhood, he simply wasn't going to set up any interviews for me—and he didn't. He told me he was weary of white folks from afar dropping into McKinley County, New Mexico, a bunch of carpetbaggers in wooden shoes, to get stories simply to please other white folks hundreds of miles away.

Broadly defined, a *carpetbagger* is someone who walks into a place, gets what he or she wants, then glibly departs. Native folks know the type well, I'm sure. Like it or not, when I wrote this book, I was a carpetbagger. Today I'm back in Sioux Center, Iowa, where I've lived for most of my life. It was my job to get stories, to write them, and, ultimately, to help readers understand the story of both the century-old mission venture many in my denomination call, somewhat erroneously, "Rehoboth," and the character and history of a proud people who were here on this continent long before white folks ever stepped foot on it.

To the Native subjects of this book, none of whom I'd ever met before, I must have seemed exactly like what Rolf Veenstra defined for me almost thirty years ago—just another Midwestern white guy on a mission from which he would soon depart and quickly return to his own easy chair.

So to all of them—the Native *and* white families included in this collection of stories—I want to say thank you, not only for consenting to be interviewed by a big, bald, white guy from afar, but for opening your lives to me as fully and lovingly as you did. You were wonderful. When I asked tough questions, you didn't flinch or toss me out of the room. You often entrusted me with some of the most intimate moments of your lives, always under the presumption that a greater, purposeful good was going to result. Perhaps what you were hoping for was simple understanding. Maybe it was the enrichment of some reader's spiritual life. Perhaps you did it because you believe in the institutions—the churches and schools associated with Rehoboth and Classis Red Mesa—that have been a part of reservation life in your neighborhoods for more than a century.

You trusted Ron Polinder when he told you I could be trusted, and then you trusted me with your stories, your hearts and souls. I can only hope—and pray too—that this collection of stories will be everything you and Ron and I wanted it to be. Inasmuch as it does succeed, it will do so only because you were willing to give me the blessings of your stories.

All of us share the faith that our lives have been eternally entrusted to the care of our mutual Savior. If your stories—and my telling of them—gain appreciative readers, let whatever good they achieve be praise to our Lord, who is our King, and the King of our families, our institutions, and every last inch of his marvelous creation.

James C. Schaap
Sioux Center, Iowa

FOREWORD

It has been a privilege for my wife, Colleen, and me to spend twenty-three years of our professional lives living among the Native American community in Northwestern New Mexico. I do not use *privilege* lightly. Living in a cross-cultural context has so enriched our life and family that we can only consider it an honor. We thank God for calling us to this adventurous and abundant life.

The privilege includes the blessing of knowing virtually all the characters in this book, except for the generation that has long ago gone to glory. We heard their stories and knew they needed to be shared. For the most part, the broader church community, along with the rest of North American society, is unfamiliar with the Native story or how the gospel took root in the Native community. It is a story quite unlike the Dutch Reformed experience of my youth, hometown, and education.

Telling these stories well requires a good storyteller, and here, too, God was well ahead of us. One day, about four years ago, I got an email from my friend Jim Schaap

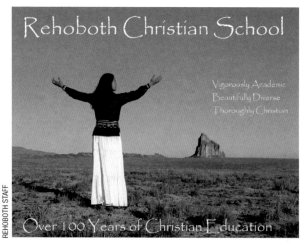

Academic, Diverse, Christian

at Dordt College. Jim was restless. He had been exploring the Lakota history and experience and had written *Touches the Sky,* a novel in which he imagines the intersection of the Sioux people and the Dutch Reformed people. He had asked me to read it in advance of publication, and I was quick to pass it on to my colleague, Rev. Stanley Jim. We both thought that Schaap got it right, not that we knew much about the Lakota story ourselves. But we knew he was able to capture the set of broader issues that haunted, and continues to haunt, these cross-cultural relationships.

Schaap's email inquired about life at Rehoboth and asked how he could help. It closed with a line to the effect that he realized that if he pushed the "send" button, his life could forever change. He did, and it has! Schaap would be the first to concur that for him also it has been a privilege to prowl around Indian country and hear these amazing stories of faith and courage and hope. It has been a delight to collaborate with Jim as we strove to gather the narratives of our Native brothers and sisters accurately, honestly, and optimistically.

Colleen and I both graduated in 1968 from Calvin College, where we gained a vision and passion for being agents of renewal in our world. God's amazing providence led us to New Mexico, where we had never been before. We started teaching in Fort Wingate, a little community with a large boarding school (1,700 boarding students in grades 1-12). While we shared the Peace Corps mentality of the 1960s, we were also intentional about wanting to be active in a church community, a desire that was fulfilled wonderfully in the smallish Fort Wingate Christian Reformed Church.

In hindsight, we recognize the paternalism we brought to our mission. Certainly, we thought, the Native people would be thrilled that we had come to teach them. After a couple of years we would once again take up our lives in "middle America." But two years became fourteen, and while we hope we were worthy of our calling as educators, we learned more from the Native people than they did from us.

What did we learn? We began to see a culture beyond textbook definitions or "mission trip" experiences. Instead we became immersed in that culture, grappling with the deepest values and issues of life. By living in a different culture, we began to understand our own.

Certain Native cultural values stood out in our experience. For instance, although we were taught the value of sharing, our Navajo friends gave that concept new meaning. If a student did not have enough money to get into a ballgame, people collectively came up with the admission. When funeral expenses came up, the extended family helped out. And the warmth and generosity of a Native potluck is unsurpassed.

And whereas my own religious tradition taught me about earthkeeping, it was an elderly Native basket weaver who demonstrated and confirmed reverence for the creation by asking permission from God to pick each reed used in a basket.

While I was taught to honor my grandparents, it wasn't until I sensed the respect my students had for their grandparents that I realized how deficient mine was. Wisdom comes from the "elderlies," as Native people say. They practice the biblical concept that gray hair is a badge of honor.

A book by John Bryde, a former Catholic priest, wonderfully captures these Native values, along with two others that are important to note: individual freedom and bravery. We observed the former value especially in how Native families reared their children, giving them a longer rope than we were inclined to give our kids—we saw, for example, third graders, and not their parents, decide whether they wanted to attend Rehoboth Christian School.

The final value Bryde mentions, bravery, is reflected in the number of Native people who serve in the military, which you'll note in these stories. In spite of confusing,

A group of Navajo Code Talkers at the dedication of the Code Talker Center at Rehoboth

conflicting, and unjust treatment of Native people by the United States government, their level of loyalty, patriotism, and sheer bravery on behalf of their country has been exemplary through the decades.

All of these lessons were rooted in our experience at Fort Wingate, where virtually all the kids spoke Navajo as their first language. Four years later, in 1972, when Colleen and I moved to Rehoboth to become dorm parents, we noticed that while our new students were wonderful kids, there was a lack of respect for the more traditional patterns. Looking back, we wish we had more aggressively challenged our students in that regard.

Not for a minute do we intend to idealize Native culture. We lived too long near Gal-

lup, "the broken glass capital of the world," and saw too much illegitimacy, alcoholism, sexual abuse, and domestic violence. We saw too much jealousy over cows, sheep, and jewelry, and we heard too much about witchcraft to believe any culture is pristine. But by God's grace, we witnessed aspects of Native culture that challenged us to live out our witness. By paying attention to what has been going on in the Native church for decades, the wider church has a splendid opportunity to learn what it means to be Christlike.

Having left New Mexico in 1982 to move back to our hometown in Lynden, Washington, we maintained our friendships by way of occasional visits, phone calls, and Christmas letters. In the summer of 1999 we returned for a longer visit and had the opportunity to look up a number of our former students. We were wonderfully blessed to see how well these "kids" were doing: many were parents now, even grandparents. They held good jobs, were leaders in their communities, and were active in their churches.

During that visit we were challenged to consider a return to the position I'd left in 1982. Rather quickly we dismissed such a notion, given our deep involvement in the education and politics and church life of our community in Washington. But there were more calls, and finally we agreed to return for a year, taking a leave of absence from Lynden Christian High School.

After the first month, Colleen and I already knew it was going to be very hard to leave. We stayed on for nine years. This time, older and wiser, we decided to live more intentionally in the Native community, worshiping in churches on the reservation, "hanging out" with Native folks, and attending events where we were often the only white folks.

We were welcomed by the community, and we marveled at the simplicity, the humor, the love, and the family commitment we witnessed. We also saw and experienced the pain that afflicts so many Native communities. But through it all, we saw faith deeper than our own and heard testimonies that made us look like beginners. Tears would well up when we heard the believers at Tohlakai Christian Reformed Church sing *Victory in Jesus* in the Navajo language.

These are the people we want you to know. Their stories will teach you, as they taught us, about faith, hope, and love.

In 2008, at a Partners Worldwide Conference, Pastor Oscar Muriu from Nairobi addressed the topic of what African Christians can contribute to the church in the West. His theme could be summed up in one word: *reciprocity*. This was not a new word to me, but it was new for me in the context of missions. It was the word I had long been searching for to characterize my experience in the Native community of New Mexico.

I realized that what had been missing from much of our mission effort in the Native community was *reciprocity*. We prevailed too much on Native people to become like the dominant culture. We lacked the humility or open-mindedness to see how Native American culture could enrich our brand of Christianity. As a result, the Native students and pastors and parishioners all too quickly felt second class and became convinced they needed to depend on the white folks to "get it right."

Rev. Stanley Jim helped me understand that the absolutely essential core value of the Native community is *respect*. In Navajo, it is *k'é* or *ił'ídlį́*. It characterizes wise, sensible, esteemed Native leaders. You will hear this value reflected in these stories: respect for the elders, respect for authority, respect for the Nation, even respect for a religion different from your own. And it is the breakdown of respect—a lack of respect for the clan, for the opposite sex, for parents, for the creation, and for self—that leads to so much grief and undermines Native culture.

Over the course of a century of mission effort in the Native community, God, in his grace and good providence, saw fit to bless the work of his stumbling servants. He honored the faithfulness of a people and a denomination who did not throw in the towel. The obstacles and challenges of transportation, housing, and health care those early missionaries faced coming to the "Wild West" in 1896 are incomprehensible

Washing up in the Rehoboth dorm

to us today. Some of the old "missionary books"—*Navajo and Zuni for Christ* and *Toiling and Trusting*—can help readers grasp the commitment, hard work, and persistence of those early missionaries. While it's easy to recognize some of their miscalculations, I am quick to ask, Who among us would be willing to walk in their shoes? These missionaries were tough and determined and faithful.

I can only guess how future generations will look back on their efforts. There are things I once said or believed that now embarrass me. Historians a couple of decades hence will find plenty of material to critique—a reminder than we need to go about our work with a serious dose of humility and respect for those who've gone before us.

One of the issues Jim Schaap and I have debated through these months is the boarding school phenomenon. You will discover in these stories the harsh realities of the boarding school—children leaving their homes as young as six years old to live in a dormitory; older kids leaving a life on the open range for a culture of regimentation and misunderstood discipline. There were casualties along the way, including plenty

of stories of abuse of various kinds from dormitory aides or "matrons," as they were often called, or by older students toward younger ones. In recognition of this painful reality, Rehoboth's hundredth anniversary celebration in 2003 included a time of confession and repentance and the publication of a "Statement of Confession and Reconciliation."

In spite of liabilities, boarding schools performed an essential role during that period of history, teaching thousands of students the essential skills they needed. Asked about their feelings and memories of their boarding school days, many students report resentment, but I have also been amazed at the resilience of many others, and even at their fond memories of boarding school days. That fondness also comes through in some of the stories.

Some parents knew they might not have enough food to eat during the winter, or enough wood to stay warm. Boarding school students testify to "three squares a day," a warm shower and bed, and some fun along the way. For many students at Rehoboth, gym time beat hauling water and chopping wood back home. On the other hand, some Native old-timers grouse about a generation of young people who don't know how to work. Parents say, "I wish I could send my kids to boarding school so they could learn how to clean."

In many cases, the boarding school dorms across the reservation were filled with loving people, some of them Christians, who cared deeply for the students. I overheard a Native woman comforting Dorothy Carlisle at her mother's funeral. Dorothy's mother, Grandma Bowman, had worked for years in the dining hall at the Tohatchi Boarding

School. This woman testified to how Mrs. Bowman showed her love for the kids by greeting them and talking to them in the cafeteria line.

I think back to Ernie and Martha Hurst, who became our *de facto* parents and mentors during our early years of teaching in Fort Wingate. Coming from pacifist Brethren roots, Ernie and Martha started working with Native students in Brigham City, Utah, as "alternative service" to a military commitment. Their temporary service became a calling. They taught us and many others to respect and honor our students and their families. We saw them live out these virtues at school, at church, and over the kitchen table playing Pinochle. We, along with the Native kids, were blessed by Ernie and Martha and dozens of others like them.

It can take years for the lessons we learn from Native culture to settle in. But there are a thousand ways for non-Natives to begin to understand, respect, admire, and learn from Native people while still being who God created us to be. Take basketball—a sport Rehoboth Christian School takes seriously. Native folks will drive for hours to see a good ballgame. Rehoboth did not have cheerleaders, and I always thought a good cheer at the right point in the game would boost our team. Through the years, I risked making a fool of myself by going out on the gym floor at a crucial moment to lead a cheer—something more typical of a loudmouthed white guy than a subdued and sensible Native. But the Native folks came to love that cheer—I think they miss it more than anything else I tried to do. The point is, they expected me to be myself— Ron Polinder—not someone else.

My passion for this project developed in part by walking around the Rehoboth cemetery with Jim Schaap. Because Colleen and I know so many of the families represented in that cemetery, the stories poured out. Too few of these stories are known outside the community, even by the Christian Reformed denomination that is so intertwined with the Native church. Native people have been part of the denomination for over a century, and many of us have barely noticed. (Another perspective, of course, is that many of us have lived within their gates since 1492.) Similarly, although most of us live in communities where Native people are our not-too-distant neighbors, they have often been disregarded or, worse, disparaged.

We are all brothers and sisters in Christ. We have much to learn from each other. My deep hope and prayer is that these stories will perk up our ears, remove scales from our eyes, and make the path toward the Native community straighter. In the process, you will receive something of the gift Colleen and I have been given—and the gift is rich!

Ron Polinder
Christmas 2009

PREFACE

Cemetery photo from cover of June 2008 *Banner*

JAMES C. SCHAAP

Most white folks would say the cemetery at Rehoboth is not a well-kept place. Yet months after Memorial Day, more adornments festoon the burial sites, per capita, than at almost any graveyard off the reservation. A miniature basketball and hoop sit on the grave of a young woman who only a year earlier had helped her Gallup team to a state championship, half-empty bottles of Coke lie half-buried in the dirt, and there are stuffed animals galore, along with ceramic angels, all kinds of toys, rosary beads hanging from a homemade wooden cross jammed into the ground beside a small statue of Mary in a Navajo blanket, and hundreds—maybe thousands—of plastic flowers.

Arlington National Cemetery's impressive orderliness makes the soldiers buried there appear to remain heroic and selfless. But at Rehoboth cemetery the dead are remembered individually, strikingly, memorably. Everywhere you look there is personality. So many stories. So much sadness. So much faith.

Here's a young woman knifed to death by her ex-boyfriend. There's the daughter of a missionary—six years old, a VanderMeulen, who died in 1948. Off to the left there, that little gray stone marks the body of baby Polinder, stillborn in 1970—one of the last deaths in the old Rehoboth hospital.

There's Albert Henry, war hero, assistant pastor at the Naschitti church, and just beyond him Sidney Nez, a missionary at Toadlena. Both were World War II Navajo Code Talkers. There's Ben Musket, whose family has been part of the Rehoboth story for four generations. There's Marie Davis, who worked in the Rehoboth kitchen for years, and Juke Den Bleyker, faithful maintenance man for even longer.

Over there is the grave of a kid who played basketball as well as anybody else in the last thirty years—he died of the effects of alcoholism. And Coolidge Begay, an almost lifelong member of Bethany Christian Reformed Church, a quiet man whose son was a sheriff and today has a great-grandson in the sixth grade at the new middle school. There's David Charles, just nineteen years old, who died in a car accident.

In a straight line running north and south are the graves of people that Christian Reformed folk might have seen in *The Banner*: the Reverend L. P. Brink, pioneer missionary who came to the shadow of the Red Rocks in 1901 and died here in '36. Rolf Veenstra, a patriarch of more recent vintage: his stone, flat and tan and somehow perfect for this desert landscape, calls him a saint. Casey Kuipers and his wife, Martha, who spent a lifetime in Zuni talking to folks about Jesus. Jessica Cameron Mierop Basie, 1913-1997, who spent some years here too.

You'll find more Navajo Code Talkers here, authentic World War II heroes, distinguished warriors whose Native tongue was indecipherable to the Japanese. And their wives too, beloved grandmas who stayed home and prayed—scores of them. There are Damons and Oppenhuizens, Henrys and Bosschers, Kamps and Begays, Yazzies and Boumas.

The rutted path down the middle of the cemetery may once have been a line of demarcation, although it is no longer. To the west, dozens of Navajo graves lie side by side, as colorful as a reservation sunset. To the right stands a line of missionary graves as poised as any synodical committee. But even though the sites are integrated now, it's the Native gravesites that lend the place its color and personality against the dusky earth tones of the desert. Keepsakes are everywhere— toy cars on the grave of a six-year-old, a boom box on a stone honoring a father, a dozen toy sheep and goats grazing over the hillside mound of a beloved grandma. Dozens of the memorials are handmade; there are lots of wooden crosses. Rehoboth cemetery looks nothing at all like a graveyard in Hull or Hudsonville or Hoboken.

Everywhere you look there are clumps of wild grasses—weedy and whiskery and seemingly out of control, snakeweed and larkspur, a scratchy profusion that would

Rehoboth cemetery

have to be hacked away or mowed down with a brush hog.

There are saints and sinners, along with what seems like a whole schoolyard of children way too young to die. All precious in God's sight.

"Four of the children whom we had learned to love and cherish are sleeping in their graves," Cocia Hartog wrote in 1910, in *Indian Mission Sketches*, not even a decade after the Rehoboth land was purchased. "It was only two weeks after her baptism that Etta Becenti died without fear," Hartog says, "knowing in whom she believed."

If there ever was a marker for Etta Becenti's grave, it's gone now. It might have fallen victim to the relentless spring winds that make the desert landscape seem uninhabitable—the same winds that erase the names of kids who've carved their initials in the sandstone rock up there on the hill to the east, beside a newer grave—Christopher Charles Johnson, a helicopter pilot killed in Iraq. His dad taught at the school.

Almost a century ago, Cocia Hartog wrote that Native people suffered from "a great fear of death." She described cultural rituals that, in some cases, have changed significantly, but still linger: "When one is about to die, the relatives usually forsake him and leave him to die alone," Hartog wrote. "The horse of the deceased is killed at the grave while his blanket, beads, or other valuables are buried with him."

I don't know if there are horses buried here, but there certainly are beads and other valuables.

On the slope at the eastern edge, five rows of white crosses stand, fatigued as war-weary sentries. There are forty or more, some of their comrades already broken or fallen. In a cemetery as heavily decorated as this is with American flags, it's impossible not to think of those crosses as marking something military. But they bear no names. They were placed there long after the original burials to mark the graves of Native people brought to the mission to die. Through many of its early years, Rehoboth Christian Hospital inherited dozens of suffering souls whose lives were at an end— sickly men and women delivered to their doorstep out of the very fear Ms. Hartog described.

At Rehoboth there were rules for Christian burials, just as there were rules at cemeteries all over the continent back then, rules long since loosened. It's quite likely that no one knows how many dead are buried beneath the tawny soil. For every stone still standing, every wooden cross in those lines, how many more markers are long gone?

The joy is that they are all here together—all these people, all these stories.

Even though the stories you will read in this book often touch upon the lives of men and women and even children buried here in the Rehoboth cemetery, these stories are primarily about the living. What the extravagant display around these graves makes clear is that those who've already passed into eternity have not been forgotten.

But then, almost any story about us has to start with our ancestors. We are who we are, in part, because of who they were. So these stories move back and forth between generations of believers to tell tales of God's abiding faithfulness. The weave of New Mexico generations creates an intricate tapestry, colored by grace into a rich testimony of the love of God—a tapestry that comes by way of a long relationship between Anglo and Native people that began more than a century ago.

In light of the difficult stories of Native missions in North America, a century of commitment seems like almost forever. Yet it would be hard to find any single square inch of territory in all this open country that tells the story better than the Rehoboth cemetery. Its silence testifies to the persistence of faith, the commitment of men and women, Native and Anglo, who have sought to bring the Good News to the people we used to call "our Indian cousins." Looking back, it's clear that not all of these efforts were as blessed as we white folks might have thought.

But just think of this: someday—maybe soon, maybe not—a trumpet will sound, and the dead will be raised incorruptible. Someday the brush will fall back and Rehoboth cemetery will come alive.

Stand out there yourself some morning in the bright New Mexico sun. Stand out there alone and marvel at what that day will bring: in the twinkling of an eye, graves—even the ones that are unmarked—will be opened for a host of witnesses stepping out of the desert dust in a blaze of silver and turquoise. Imagine them—men and women, boys and girls, ancients and stillborn—all singing together in a chorus of Navajo, English, Zuni, Dutch, and Spanish—a chorus of praise.

From the new church at Rehoboth or the brand-new school gym, it takes no more than fifteen minutes to walk to the cemetery—maybe a half-mile due south of the old Mission House. Go out by yourself some bright morning and wander through the plots. Sift through the stories; take note of the love and care all around. Make it a pilgrimage. And then dream of graves razed, the whole place suddenly opened.

"Never again will there be an infant who lives but a few days, or an old man who does not live out his years," says the prophet Isaiah.

Every knee shall bow. Every tongue confess.

That's been the vision of Rehoboth for more than one hundred years. We hope the very human stories in this book will bring us all closer to the God who rules us and who loves us eternally.

CHAPTER 1

Very Much at Home

Louise and Bennie Musket

That Louise and Bennie Musket would someday fall in love and marry wasn't much of a surprise. Sure, there were five years between them—Louise is that much younger—but she already had eyes for Bennie when she was in junior high. Even if Louise tries to deny it, Bennie has not forgotten and he'll tell you so, smiling the way he does—at her.

Just a few miles of reservation land separated their childhood homes north of Tohlakai. Louise Belone, the third child of Harry and Lorraine, grew up just south of Charley Damon's old trading post. That's where Bennie, Charley's grandson, used to hang around drinking sodapop and making himself the kind of nuisance little boys often do. Bennie, the fourth child of Bah Damon and Benjamin Musket, grew up another mile or two north on land where he and Louise still live today.

There was little separating them, really, just a few years and a few miles. So they found each other, got married, raised their own family, herded sheep, and now have spent more

What remains of Charley Damon's store

than forty years together on a slice of reservation land that's home to both of them.

But, if the truth be known, more links them than neighborhood and birth. Bennie Musket and Louise Belone grew up in the households of strong parents whose dedicated will and sheer devotion created unforgettable impressions in their lives. Both had parents who made their values as clear as a New Mexico morning sky.

Navajo Code Talkers at the dedication of the Rehoboth Code Talker Center

Harry Belone

"My dad was a pusher," Louise will tell you. "'Go to school—go to school. That's the only way you'll make something of yourself,' he used to say. When everybody was there—like Thanksgiving and Christmas, he would talk to all of us. 'Go to school,' he'd say."

Louise's father, Harry Belone, didn't just talk the talk. After he retired, he went to Gallup himself and got his GED. Yes, you read that right—*after* he retired, he went back to school. He'd gone earlier in his life, before many other Navajo boys had, in fact. He spent several years at Tohatchi Boarding School, then was sent off to the Phoenix Indian School, where he finished grade school.

That's where his education ended because that's about the time World War II began. Off went Harry Belone, Sr., to the South Pacific. There, along with his Marine buddies, he hopped, skipped, and jumped from island to island, fighting the Japanese in combat that seemed as vicious as it did unending.

Harry Belone no longer lives in his neighborhood just off the 6-6-6, the road people used to call "The Devil's Highway." His residence is in a wholly other place—on high. But even today, Harry Belone is a hero, not just to his children, his grandchildren, and his great-grandchildren; but to Navajos especially and to all American people. Harry Belone came back from those bloody battles on Pacific islands with a Purple Heart, having lost a significant part of his vision to some kind of incendiary device. But he was also among those who were called "Code Talkers"—Navajo warriors who used their native tongue to deceive the best and brightest Japanese code-breakers. Harry Belone was a war hero.

After some rehabilitation in San Francisco for his injuries, he returned to the reservation to his wife, Lorraine, and their three kids, including daughter Louise, whom he had never before seen (Lorraine was pregnant with her at the time he had left). He came home to a job at the Fort Wingate ammunitions depot, and he became a growing presence in the local Navajo tribal chapter and in the tribe itself.

When Harry Belone spoke, people listened—including his own children. When he told them they had to have an education, they heard the directive. When Louise finished high school at Gallup, her father told her that wasn't enough. "You've got to learn something," he said, meaning a job or trade. So off she went to Albuquerque for secretarial work, part of what was called at the time the "Relocation" program, which was set up and run by the Bureau of Indian Affairs.

"That's where Bennie found me," she says, chuckling a little and looking at him.

Bah Damon

Bennie Musket also grew up with a strong and determined parent—his mother, Bah, who was no war hero but has her own amazing story.

Bah's father, Charley Damon, is almost legendary among people who live in the Gallup area. During the early decades of the twentieth century, Charley Damon had 5,000 sheep—that alone was enough to make him legendary. His daughter Bah inherited from her father a similarly enterprising charac-

ter. When she was 82 years old, she still insisted on being out in the hills and desert, tending sheep on horseback. Throughout her life she always had sheep. She was a foreman in her father's huge operation at a time when few women held such positions. Plenty of men worked under her, including, for a time at least, her second husband—Bennie Musket's father.

Navajo woman tending sheep

MARV SWARTZ

The Damon family is bountifully represented in the history of Rehoboth. Charley himself acted as one of the very first mission interpreters, a Native speaker who would accompany the early missionaries on their forays onto the reservation. Those pastors—Freyling, Vander Wagen, Brink, as well as a second generation, with names like Vander Stoep and Kamps—would ride out to the hogans of the people. Accompanied by a Native speaker and translator, they'd walk up to doorways and ask to chat, to bring the

Dr. Richard Pousma with a young patient

In the spring, dusty winds can just about choke man and beast. On one of those long and cold overnights during the 1930s, Shay Etcitty caught something akin to pneumonia and died, leaving Bah alone with their two kids—a boy and a girl. Shay, too, was definitely something of a hero of faith.

During her husband's hospitalization at Rehoboth, Bah found her way into the lives of some of the folks there, including Dr. Richard Pousma, who couldn't help but admire her will and her strength of character. In fact, even though Bah had no medical training, Pousma asked her if she would work with him as a surgical nurse because, he told her, she was not in the least squeamish and was blessed with a tenacious strength of character.

Bah made it very clear to her son Bennie that an education was essential—a requirement for her children (which was remarkable, considering that she didn't have an education herself). That admonition normally came with an appraisal of her own life's work—keeping sheep. This is how Bennie remembers her saying it: "'Sheep is hard work,' she used to tell us," he says. "'Sheep is hard work.' That's why she sent all the kids down there to Rehoboth to be educated. 'Hey, sheep is hard work.'"

And there was more. "In order to get ahead in life, you've got to get an education," Bennie remembers Bah saying. But then she'd widen the command. "'It doesn't have to be from high school or college,' she'd tell us, because she'd say, "you could get an education elsewhere, just in life itself. But sheep is hard work.'"

Bennie, like his brother and sister before him, attended Rehoboth for several years, right up until junior high. Then he decided, like other young guys, he says, that he

gospel. Because Charley Damon acted as an interpreter for those early missionaries, the Christian Reformed Church has been a part of Bennie Musket's family history for five generations, from Grandpa Charley to Louise and Bennie's three grandchildren—two now graduated and two (Jeannette and Megan) still enrolled at Rehoboth.

Bah Damon Musket's first husband, Shay Etcitty, was also a translator for early CRC missionaries. Family history tells the story of his death this way. Often, as Shay accompanied a missionary preacher on his travels around the wide-ranging Navajo reservation, they'd need to bed down under the stars, having no where else to sleep. That sounds more storied—more TV Western-ish—than it often was. During monsoon season, a storm can transform an ordinary parched gulch into whitewater madness in minutes.

wanted football more than Rehoboth. So he quit—but he never forgot those early years.

If you know a little about each of their family backgrounds—specifically about their parents—it's not at all difficult to understand how Louise Belone and Bennie Musket started making eyes at each other when they were kids, and how their love has lasted for 48 years.

Bennie and Louise

But there's more to the story than hard work and accomplishment. Every generation changes. We're all someone's child, but no child is a clone. We all have to find our own way because the Lord God Almighty simply doesn't bring in whole family lines. He's interested in each of us as individuals.

Bennie Musket had to wait for Louise Belone—after all, he was five years older. Once he graduated from high school in Gallup, he took a job in Tuba City, Arizona, at a uranium processing plant where he handled materials in a fashion that today would be considered highly dangerous. His work cycle was to be in that plant for three weeks of hard labor, then get a week off to go back home to Mexican Springs.

After a year, he too applied to the BIA Relocation program and was sent to Cleveland, Ohio, to learn the welding trade (he'd seen how important welders were in the plant in Tuba City). Relocation was a government program designed to help Native people make the considerably difficult move off reservations; it was undertaken at a time when thousands of Native people were leaving reservations all over the country. The government provided pay ($40 per week), enrollment in a technical school, and a place to live. The school's program usually provided for internships.

Bennie Musket in uniform

In Cleveland, Bennie learned the welder's trade, but the intention of the program—to acclimate a Native kid to a place *off* the reservation—failed. He didn't care for the big city and returned to the reservation.

Life in the Marines

By the time Bennie returned, the military draft wanted him badly and was threatening incarceration if he didn't report (he hadn't received their letters while he was in Ohio). At the last minute, along with a cousin, he decided to enlist in the Marines rather than report to the Army because a recruiter promised them all sorts of goodies. Those bonuses never materialized.

His relationship with Louise, who was still finishing up high school, moved into long-distance mode. When Louise describes that time, she mimics writing letters, something she did regularly during the four-and-one-half years Bennie spent in the service.

Bennie's Marine experience had a significant effect on their lives together. For most of those years, he was almost pleasantly stationed in perfectly peaceful areas of the world, from Japan to the Mediterranean. But the final eight months he spent in Vietnam.

It was 1965, and the war effort was not yet what it would become just a few years later. Regardless, Bennie's deployment there was dangerous and scary. By day, the heavy-equipment training he'd received after basic training kept him at the controls of caterpillars and road graders just outside DaNang. But at night, his infantry platoon was responsible for guard duty, during which, he says, he never felt much fear at all, even though the area was growing more dangerous all the time.

It wasn't until he was leaving Vietnam that something hit him—the fear he had for so long simply put out of mind. Like so many Vietnam vets, he returned home unsettled, even broken. Today Bennie describes himself this way: "I was kind of unstable then—being in the Marine Corps and all of that, and I lost my fellowship with God."

And he almost lost Louise too. She was asking herself whether or not she really wanted this man who seemed so deeply altered by his military experience. But by that time there was a daughter, Lorenda, and there was a commitment that she had no desire to break.

If you charted the faith life of Bennie and Louise Musket, those days and months when Bennie returned from service would be at the bottom of the graph. Things were in bad shape, especially for Bennie. Everyone told him as much, including his mother, who said in no uncertain terms that nothing—not an education, not anything—mattered as much as his relationship to Jesus Christ. She did everything she could to get him to see that he had to bring his life back in line with the truth he knew so well in his heart—that Jesus Christ was his Lord and Savior.

The Miracle of Rebirth

And that's exactly what happened. Almost miraculously, one Sunday when the two of them were together in the Tohatchi church ("she used to go more than I did at that time," he says), Bennie heard a sermon by Pastor Charlie Gray. He determined, on his own, that the instability he'd felt in his soul and showed in his life simply had to end. He resolved to put the drinking, the restlessness, and the lack of peace behind him—and he did it on his own. No counseling, no treatment, just simple resolve powered exclusively by a commitment to the truth of the gospel.

Of course, to say he did it on his own is a good deal less than a half-truth. Bennie Musket brought order to his life—and his family's life—upheld by the prayers of all kinds of friends and relatives who pleaded daily for the change that blessedly happened in his life. It was the God of heaven and earth—of DaNang and Mexican Springs—who came into Bennie's heart and spirit.

When he wrote about that day a few years later in an edition of *The Christian Indian*, he described it this way: "We experienced one of the most wonderful days of our lives. We confessed the Lord Jesus as our Lord and Savior. Louise and our two children were baptized. We are now one in Him with all those He has confessed before the Father."

Had he simply forgotten the promises of the Lord that he had learned at Rehoboth Christian School? No. "The Lord used [Pastor Charley Gray's] message to wake up my faith," he wrote in that article. At Rehoboth, a foundation in faith was created, so that when he and Louise determined to send their own children to school there, the motivation arose from his belief in the education he himself had received. "To me," he says, "Rehoboth is a second home, even though I got out of there to play football. I know what it is, why it's there. It's the beginning of my faith in the Lord Jesus. I knew Jesus from there. Even though there were hard times, Rehoboth laid the groundwork."

As Bennie and Louise grow older, their faith grows only stronger. They find themselves coming ever closer to the Lord.

Ten years ago, their youngest daughter, Melvina, who today works in the development office at Rehoboth, contracted one of the deadliest and least understood viruses in the world—the hantavirus. For the afflicted, there simply is no cure. How Melvina contracted the virus remains a mystery; that she had it is something she and her family will never forget.

In just a few short days, Melvina went from being just a bit tired to being deathly ill. The doctors' major task was keeping her heart beating. There were moments in the I.C.U. of the University of New Mexico Hospital when the doctors and nurses told Bennie and Louise and many other family members to expect the worst; it seemed that the trajectory of Melvina's life was moving toward its imminent close.

One day, when the outlook was especially dim, the prayers of dozens of believers arose like a mighty flood. Louise will never forget it. "One of my nieces called the

JOY BURMEISTER

Melvina Musket

prayer line, and the preacher called people and told them all to get together and pray. It was 11:00 in the morning," she says, as if the prayers themselves were a miracle. "We were praying too, all of us, in the chapel at the hospital."

"They were all praying—all of them," Melvina herself adds. "And then I got better."

It's as shocking a story today as it was then. The killer virus was suddenly slain.

"We couldn't believe it. Just a few hours earlier they had said there was little hope," Louise says. "By three, it was over."

Together, all those who'd gathered at the hospital went to the chapel and gave collective thanks for the life of Melvina Musket. She went from life to near death to life again—all in a matter of three days. After

Louise and Bennie Musket

some additional recovery time she was released on May 10, 1998—Mother's Day.

Because the hantavirus had been in their home, everything in the Musket house had to be cleaned—everything. For a week afterward, Louise worked at washing bedding and towels and lifting rugs. "I was so tired," she remembers. Even today, ten years later, tears come to her eyes when she remembers.

"And all of a sudden the Lord spoke to me," she says. "He said, 'Mrs. Musket, you would be packing those clothes.' And I just hung on to whatever I was hanging, and I said, 'Yes, Lord, I would have.' And that was it. I just said, 'Thank you, Lord, for giving her back to me.'"

That's how close Louise and Bennie Musket are to the Maker of heaven and earth.

Home

In the old days, Navajo mothers would bury their children's umbilical cords in the earth near the hogans where those children were brought into this world. It was a ritual designed not only to nurture a living bond between the land itself and the human beings who were blessed to live upon it, but also to give each child a sense of home.

Today, Louise and Bennie Musket live on Musket land, where they—like Bennie's mother—still have sheep. Just down the road, where they always have been, live Louise's family, her people. It's as though the two of them never left home.

They did leave, as all of us do. But today, without a doubt—just ask them—they are home on earth that is as familiar as the ritual passing of the New Mexico seasons, home in the arms of their Lord and Savior.

CHAPTER 2

Pray Without Ceasing

Elizabeth Bitsie Jones

You've got to go pretty far west in the settlement of Tohatchi, New Mexico, to find it, but First Navajo CRC is there, as it has been for a century. The fellowship itself dates even farther back; records indicate that the Tohatchi reservation settlement was first visited by a Christian Reformed missionary in 1896, when Andrew Vander Wagen traveled there from what was then the heart of the CRC mission enterprise in Ft. Defiance, Arizona.

The remarkable old church standing at the west edge of town wasn't built until 1910, probably under the auspices of Christian Reformed churches in and around Holland, Michigan, who had, so history suggests, taken it upon themselves to build a church not unlike their own.

J. D. De Korne's book *Navajo and Zuni for Christ* (1947) features an old, blurry winter picture of the Tohatchi church. Snow drapes its roof and its nearby parsonage, making the hills that stand just beyond them completely invisible. Without those hills, that old church building could be mistaken

First Navajo CRC, known today as Tohatchi CRC

for a church in any of a dozen Dutch-immigrant hamlets ridiculously far removed from New Mexico's high plains.

That early missionaries carted their own distinctive Anglo cultures along to the reservations is an argument that doesn't require much proof. The design of First Navajo CRC is a symbol of both the strengths and weaknesses of early mission enterprise,

25

not simply that of the CRC but of every other Anglo denominational effort. The significant gift of a typical West Michigan church building, complete with functional basement, is as stunning in its heartfelt beneficence as it is in its cultural blindness.

But that old church, no matter whose design it is or was, is absolutely central to the life and the story of Elizabeth Bitsie Jones. She's lived every one of her seventy years right there in the neighborhood, a resident of the nearby settlement of Mexican Springs. All of her life she's attended First Navajo CRC, shepherded there as a child along with eight brothers and sisters by her God-fearing parents, Walter B. and Freida (Upshaw) Bitsie. Elizabeth herded her own eleven kids there. Even today, with her children grown and married themselves, she's still there every week, often twice, encircled by her beloved family.

Elizabeth Bitsie Jones never really left First Navajo CRC or the neighborhood. In the mid-twentieth century, when Elizabeth was born and reared on the reservation, it was the custom of most Navajo families to expand the family compound when the family itself expanded. One frame-house would become two and three and four. Growing up in a compound with a medley of related families, like Elizabeth did, only makes the relatedness more intimate. So while a nephew of hers now lives in the house Elizabeth grew up in, she still lives just down the path—as do several other closely related families.

If you visit Tohatchi CRC you'll meet a goodly number of her family members, a brother or a sister or two or three, as well as her children and theirs, scattered throughout the old wooden pews. And when they sing—which they love to do—you'll hear the voices of that extended family, just as you would have in the old church a half-century or more ago.

Elizabeth Bitsie Jones's family loves to make music, in part, because of another largely Anglo cultural artifact: an instrument that still makes music in the old family compound, still standing in a Bitsie home—a piano. It's altogether possible that when Elizabeth's father, Walter Bitsie, bought a piano and brought it to the house years ago, you would have had to look far and wide to find another Navajo home so graced. Family lore, Elizabeth says, maintains that her father paid $50 for the piano, no paltry sum in the early years of the twentieth century.

What Elizabeth herself will never forget—and what her own children remember fondly—is standing around that piano and singing, mostly hymns, with brother Wilsie's fingers dancing up and down the keyboard while mother Frieda accompanied on the harmonica.

Similar scenes played out in hundreds of Dutch CRC families of the era, but with one notable difference. Many Native cultures were, even well into the twentieth century, largely oral in nature. Narratives, admonitions, and testimonies were passed along in a family circle. It was part of a family's way of life, part of the musical ritual the Bitsies reveled in. Rather than allowing children to dominate family conversation, Navajos, like many other Native people, gave center stage to the elderly, who regularly held forth on how to live.

Elizabeth's son, Marvin, remembers how those life lessons were passed along: "Grandma used to sing with us and tell us stories about Jesus, and that piano was always there," he says. "Grandma played the harmonica and would tell us to sing, and they'd tell us stories about the Lord—what messages she'd heard and the way of life of Jesus. It was quite a testimony."

Around that old piano, that Anglo icon, a very traditional Navajo custom was passed along—the elders speaking to the children about a way of life, which for the Bitsies meant a Christian way of life.

But just how did Elizabeth Bitsie Jones come to believe in Jesus Christ as her Savior? If you ask her, she'll answer by talking about her father, Walter, who for a time was a translator for the church and the Rehoboth mission, and who remained a devoted Christian throughout his life. His faith began when he was barely a man, at a time when his grieving father asked him to do something he simply couldn't, or wouldn't. It began as an urge—a deep, unsettled feeling about a custom he simply wouldn't abide.

The Death of a Brother

It's an ancient story now, and telling it, as Elizabeth does, requires some Navajo history, because even among Native people the Navajo regard for death appears to be uniquely their own. According to Raymond Friday Locke, in *The Book of the Navajo*, "Death and everything connected with it is repulsive . . . and dead humans are buried as quickly as possible." Locke says that, traditionally, the Navajo people had no vision of heaven or of some sweet afterlife. Once departed, the dead are met at the bottom of a mountain trail by relatives they recognize, who then guide them toward the underworld.

What remains, the corpse, was considered horrid to many traditional Navajo. In *Blood and Thunder: An Epic of the American West*, Hampton Sides says it is ironic that the Navajo were greatly feared by their neighbors, since "the Navajos avoided killing whenever possible because theirs was a culture that had a deep-seated fear and revulsion of death. They wanted nothing to do with corpses or funerals or anything connected with mortality."

The story Elizabeth Jones's father, Walter Bitsie Sr., used to tell her about his acceptance of the Christian faith is a story about death and custom and culture—and a story about life.

"My dad always told us that somehow he became a child of God through his little brother," she says. "When he was growing up, my grandparents lost one of his brothers—my dad's brother—and he was told to take him up in the hills and bury him up there. That was a tradition that they grew up with."

Of great concern was the disposal of the body because in the early years of the twentieth century and for as far back as anyone could remember, the dangerous spirits of the dead were thought to rise from the corpse. Walter Bitsie did as his father asked. "He said he took his little brother up there and put his body on a tree or a rock—I don't remember which," she says. "Then he came home."

But what he'd done bothered him, even though bringing his little brother's body out toward the hills was what his father had asked him to do. He couldn't get over the irritation he felt, the guilt.

A day or two later, he went to the trading post. The trader, Mr. Garcia, a Mexican and a Roman Catholic, told him that leaving his brother's body up there on a rock or a tree just wasn't right. "'You bring him back, and I'll buy you the lumber and make a box, and we'll put him away in the right way,'" Mr. Garcia told him.

Dr. Richard Pousma does some dental work out in the open.

"So my father said that he did that," Elizabeth explains, nodding as though she is swearing this is the truth as she herself heard it from her father a dozen times, maybe even more around that piano. "He had to undress himself at that point because of the stigma of the dead person. So he did, and he built a coffin with his own hands, and brought his brother's body back down, put it in the coffin, and buried him in a little cemetery at the foot of the hills. The trader got him the lumber, and he made the coffin."

All of this Walter did on his own, on the sly, because he did not want his parents to know what he'd done. After all, they were very traditional, she says, and "cemeteries weren't the way of the traditional Navajos at the time. It would have been wrong." He listened to his conscience, but he also respected his father.

So rather than face his parents and tell the truth, Walter walked away from the hogan at Mexican Springs. "He left for California rather than tell his parents what he did. He left. Went to California, went to school at that time."

But there is more to the story. "When he came back from California—months were like years back then, it seems," she says, "—his parents asked about the body. He thought they would have forgotten about it, but they asked him—and then he told them." He told them he'd disobeyed them, that he had followed a new way, a Christian way, and a higher authority.

But there's still more to the story. Trader Garcia wasn't the one who offered

Walter Bitsie his first taste of Christianity. Dr. Richard Pousma, from the Rehoboth mission, had visited with him often. "Doc Pousma inspired my dad," Elizabeth says. "He used to come with the wagon and visit, wherever people would live, bring clothes for the kids and say a prayer for them. He went out, being a doctor, rather than having the people just go to Gallup."

Her grandfather, Walter's father, a Navajo medicine man, never once came to church in all his life, at least not that Elizabeth knows of. He was very traditional, and Christianity meant such an unthinkably significant change. But he understood that things were changing around him. While he had passed along his medicinal and spiritual craft to his son, the old man recognized that things were not going to stay as they had always been.

Once when Elizabeth's father was beginning to craft a ritual for a sick child in traditional ways, she remembers, "He sang over a little girl, and then he said that his own dad stopped him and told him, 'No, don't do that anymore.'" That's how Elizabeth remembers her father telling the story. The old medicine man encouraged his son to move his heart and soul in a different direction because he understood that the old ways were not going to be sufficient for the people he both loved and served. While he could never become a Christian himself, Walter Bitsie's father graciously gave his son leave to follow the lead given him by his own heart and soul and by the gospel offered by Dr. Pousma.

Maybe what happened to Walter Bitsie was not at all like Damascus Road; yet what happened to him was deeply and powerfully related because accepting the Christian gospel created a radical change in what he recognized himself to be and the way he lived his life.

Elizabeth Bitsie Jones was born in 1941, the seventh of nine children, all of them reared in a devotedly Christian home on the family compound just outside Mexican Springs. She was heir to a powerful faith and commitment evidenced in what her parents said and in what they did. She is, as some might say, a seventy-year-old covenant child, a woman who doesn't remember a time when God's Word itself wasn't a vivid presence in her life.

All of which doesn't mean, of course, that her life has been either a bowl of cherries or a bed of roses. She married a good man who rarely darkens the door of First Navajo CRC. Her own children have logged some miles through the dark valleys many good folks on the reservation enter; and when such things have happened, she has been herself a stronghold, an ever-present source of hope and trust and abiding faith in God's promises. Some call her a saint, but she wouldn't see it that way herself.

Lost and Found

Son Marvin, the third of those eleven kids, remembers a time when he woke up in his Chevy S-10 Blazer and found its rear end bashed in from an accident he didn't remember having. He'd been drinking heavily while on the road for his job.

He was on his way back home when something changed, he says. "I was coming back. I was so miserable, had a hangover, and at the same time, there was fear in me that I'd put my job in jeopardy." But it wasn't his job that brought on the darkness. It was what he was doing to his wife, Janice, and his new daughter. "I needed a savior," he says. "I was all by myself, when all that stuff came into my head—that something has to happen in my life. I was just thinking—miserable, praying. 'I can't do this on my own. I can't do this myself.'" And then he spoke to God. "'I know you're there because I heard about you long ago, for most of my life,'" he remembers, "'and I heard about what can happen if I just lay down my life. I know I failed you.'"

He got off the road near Ganado; he says he "couldn't help but stop." He went through a gate and got far enough off the road so no one would see him, then "pulled up and just cried. I sat there for a half hour. 'I've had it with what I'm doing,'" he told the Lord. "'I'm blowing it. I need your help. I can't go on this way.'" Then, he says, he felt relieved.

Back home, he told his wife, Janice, the whole story. Although she was from a very traditional family up north, she had been coming to First Navajo CRC faithfully, along with her mother-in-law, Elizabeth, both women attending even when their husbands did not.

Many Christians like their stories neatly tied in a sacramental bow, but some are not so beautifully presented. When Janice heard the full recitation of her husband's drunken mess, after she'd listened to him and even seen his tears, she says she was skeptical. She says she didn't believe him.

And that wasn't surprising, because Marvin slipped off the wagon again not all that long thereafter. And again. And again. Each time, after confessing his need to be clean, to be washed in the blood of the Lamb—each time he claimed it wouldn't happen again. And through all of this, Janice and her mother-in-law kept going back to First Navajo CRC,

Elizabeth, Marvin, and Janice Jones

Display at Rehoboth Code Talker Center

where the two of them would, once again, take up the armor of faithful prayer warriors.

Elizabeth says that through all that warfare with alcohol, she always continued to pray for Marvin—"ongoing prayer," she calls it, prayer without ceasing. And she would talk to him, not only about his drinking, but about other things. "And then Jan and I shared a lot, too," she explains. "We always prayed a lot about things," because, one might say, the Lord was their refuge, their stronghold.

Prayer Will Take Care of It

Elizabeth Bitsie Jones claims she has never lost faith, even when her children seemed to. Her persistent love means never shutting the door. "I never just jump all over them," she says, "because prayer will take care of it." She tells her children who've seemingly left the faith, "There will come a time when you will cry out to the Lord."

Now, at seventy, she still has a calling to fulfill and she knows it. "I worry about all of them—and especially my grandkids, especially these days. Each and every night I sit in my living room and I pray about them—all of them." Sometimes she fears, she says, that they're not all in the fold. The pressures of the world are substantial, sometimes even terrifying, but she's learned, she says, "to just leave it up to the Lord."

But she has good reason to trust that Lord. Her big brother Wilsie, the piano player, attended Rehoboth school through the eighth grade, which was as far as it went in those days. He was a decorated war hero, a Navajo code talker, one of the original 29 in the Pacific Theater of the Second World War. He returned from the war and played the piano, time and time again, for funerals and weddings. Wilsie was a widely-known character around Tohatchi and Mexican Springs. But he left the church and went back to a more traditional Navajo way of life, holding little but disdain for the Christian faith, the white man's religion.

But Elizabeth watched that same big brother reclaim on his deathbed the faith so many had thought he'd given up completely, the faith he'd seen in the open and trusting lives of his own mother and father.

"Yes, I was there," she remembers fondly. "He even jumped off his bed and he walked, when he couldn't even walk again. I was happy and I hugged him." A month later, after coming back to the Christian faith, Wilsie was gone.

Elizabeth Bitsie Jones knows who to trust.

Rehoboth

Elizabeth's brother Calvin went to Rehoboth school, as did a couple other older siblings back in the 1940s. But for some reason, by the time Elizabeth grew into school age, Rehoboth was no longer an option, so she didn't go herself. She says she thinks the decision was a matter of money. Instead, she followed her mother, who worked as a matron at the Tohatchi boarding school. None of her own eleven children attended Rehoboth either.

But today, the number of Jones grandchildren who have attended or graduated or are still there takes some time to compute. There are many. Oddly enough, it was Janice who inaugurated the move toward Rehoboth. It was Janice, the daughter-in-law who was not reared in a Christian family, whose husband gave her every reason to write out her own sorry verses of a country-western tune. It was Janice who talked Marvin, her husband, into sending their kids to a Christian school, to Rehoboth. It was Janice who opened the floodgates for the legion of Jones family grandkids.

And what of Marvin, her husband through all these years? "He always tells his kids and tells me that he's happy where his children are, and that he can't ask for anything more. 'I'm just happy where they all are,' he says, and he always tells me thank you for being strong for them."

The smile on Elizabeth Jones's face seems as healthy as it does, no doubt, because in so many ways this covenant child has learned to wait on the Lord, to let him find the way through. She's learned to put all her fear and anxiety into God's generous hands.

Not long ago one Sunday evening, her son Marvin held forth at First Navajo CRC in Tohatchi. Marvin's been on the wagon far more than he's been off in the last ten years. These days the pulpit belongs to him on the occasional Sunday. He's an energetic preacher and singer, his mother's child.

One such Sunday started off with lots of singing—loud and proud singing. And then Marvin opened the Word to the famous passage from Ephesians 6, where the apostle Paul turns us all into warriors: "Stand firm then, with the belt of truth buckled around your waist, with the breastplate of righteousness in place, and with your feet fitted with the readiness that comes from the gospel of peace." What Marvin preached on that night, in a church that is a century old, was the importance of wearing God's own armor in the warfare all of us face every day of our lives—a war to be waged, as Paul says, with the least likely of weapons, "the gospel of peace."

It's a sermon he's seen enacted in the simple, steadfast presence of a mother who has never once stopped hoping and loving and praying.

CHAPTER 3

The Beauty Way

Ed and Dorothy Carlisle

"Throughout my life, people have asked me what I learned at Rehoboth. For want of a better answer and due to my lack of experience and limited ability to place things in larger perspective, I have usually said, 'Rehoboth gave us a strong academic foundation.' That statement was true in part but really failed to do justice to the question. Based upon my subsequent learning and life experiences, I decided to try to answer the question more fully, with the caveat that hundreds of students went through the school and may have other answers to the same question."

So begins a thoughtful memoir Ed Carlisle penned not long ago, because, he says, he wanted to explain clearly what the Rehoboth school meant to him years ago, when he was a student there, and what it means to him today, as a board member and as a grandfather of kids who still attend the school.

Fifty years ago, he says, different people would have given different answers if questioned about the mission of the Mission School. Some would have said Rehoboth's

Dorothy and Ed Carlisle

purpose was to raise up preachers from the Native people. Others would have offered different answers—"to give students an educational foundation for life," for instance, or to teach its students "the Way, the Truth, and the Life."

When he thinks back on his time at Rehoboth, Ed starts in on yet another variation: "Based upon the effectiveness of my experience at Rehoboth," he writes, "I think it can also be said that the school's mission was, in part, to give us basic tools: the ability to think rationally, to analyze, and to formulate plans to address our daily needs, professional demands, and our own life's adversities . . . to prepare students for adulthood and long-term spiritual realities and needs."

And then, in the fashion of the Christian education he received, Ed lays a foundation under that assertion, appealing to the Word of God: "When I was a child, I thought as a child, I spoke as a child, and acted as a child. But when I became a man, I put away my childish ways . . . Now we see in part, understand in part, know in part, but then we shall see [God] face to face." Ed Carlisle

would be among the first to say that often the Word of God doesn't require interpretation. But he's still too much the lawyer not to build a case. "It seems to me that Paul is saying we must learn to assume our earthly and spiritual responsibilities or face the consequences of our own childishness."

Throughout his life, among the people he's loved and served on the reservation, Ed Carlisle has seen childishness and petty selfishness. Even when he was a boy, Rehoboth Mission School, he says, prepared him for something different—for adulthood.

A Family Tree

One of Ed's cousins is hard at work creating a family tree, and she's pulling her hair out trying to locate the great-grandparents' names. There's a reason for that. A century

Andrew and Effie Vander Wagen

Missionary visits

ago and more, census takers relied on information they were told orally, and that information tended to be more than occasionally unreliable. Among Native people back then, names were changed with some regularity.

Ed Carlisle knows this much for sure: his paternal grandfather's name was Hosteen Cowboy. Hosteen was a medicine man, a traditional healer, a leader, and a wise man in the small Navajo community of Pinehaven, fifteen miles or so southeast of Gallup, at the foot of the Zuni Mountains. Ed Carlisle is proud of his grandfather's legacy of wisdom and thoughtfulness.

Throughout his adult years, Hosteen Cowboy became a trusted friend of Andrew Vander Wagen, a pioneer missionary who came to the region in 1896, and began—along with his wife, Effie—an almost legendary career that ended not in Michigan or Iowa but right there in McKinley County, New Mexico.

By the 1920s and 30s, Vander Wagen was already getting on in years, but he made regular visits to his family's trading posts throughout the region. On the days he'd visit Pinehaven, where Ed grew up, Vander Wagen would stop off to chat with the venerable Hosteen Cowboy. Sitting in the shade on summer afternoons, the two of them could go on and on for hours, talking about religion and faith, about living right before God, about ideas they shared and ideas they didn't share. "My grandfather was a traditional healer who practiced the 'Beauty Way' and 'Life Way' ceremonies," Ed says.

For the most part, Vander Wagen let Mr. Cowboy be, even though he never stopped delivering the Word. "Vander Wagen accepted the Navajos as they were," Ed says. "He sat on the ground with them and ate roast mutton or mutton stew, tortillas or fried bread, fresh or dried corn, green beans and squash, and sometimes venison."

Despite deeply held contrary religious views, Mr. Cowboy and Mr. Vander Wagen were blessed with similar personalities. "Both men were quiet, friendly, gentle, and kind," Ed explains, "and they developed mutual understanding and respect."

Grandpa Cowboy became, in a way, a kind of missionary too, explaining the traditional Navajo religion as a way of thinking and believing and living, a way of life that stresses the importance of maintaining a balance between the individual and the universe, of living in harmony with nature and the Creator.

It was Vander Wagen who talked Grandpa Cowboy into sending his son—whose name was also Ed—off to school at Rehoboth, despite Mr. Cowboy's traditional ways. He'd come to recognize something good in Vander Wagen's teaching, something that would be of great value to his own children, Ed explains. "Grandpa told me that I was going to Rehoboth because the people there live the real 'Beauty Way.'"

In those days, Rehoboth would not have taught Navajo or Zuni children the traditional ways. But Grandpa Cowboy saw something beyond the immediate: both ways of life preached love and respect and tolerance, and for him that convergence was enough. That's how Rehoboth came to be a significant part of Ed Carlisle's life.

Rehoboth Mission School

Even though he's spent most of his life in some kind of public service—as an employee of the Navajo tribe, the Bureau of Indian Affairs, and the state of New Mexico—Ed recalls a boyhood of plain old hard work. "If you could carry only one ear of corn," he says, "then you carried one ear of corn. That's how we lived." Taking care of live-

Muddle-headed sheep!

stock, a job that fell to him too frequently, as he remembers, was not his idea of a fulfilling profession: "Sheep are the stupidest things I've ever seen, and goats are the craziest."

So when his father, who'd attended Rehoboth himself through the sixth grade, started talking about his own son going to boarding school there, it seemed like a grand idea to Ed Junior. Sadly, he didn't get in. For the first two years he applied, Ed was turned down by Rehoboth: they decided he was too small, too young to stay in the dorm. Finally his third application was accepted, and Ed happily wandered away from those muddle-headed sheep and crazy goats.

Back then, Rehoboth was a strange world to a boy or girl from the reservation, Ed says, and in some cases it still is. But he'd been prepared for the change during the two years when he was waiting to be accepted. His father told him again and again how important education was for his people. As the secretary of his tribal chapter, Ed's father frequently traveled all over the reservation visiting other chapters, sometimes on horseback, sometimes hitching rides with others (chapter officers were volunteers back then). "We need good schools," his father would tell him when the two of them were on the way somewhere or coming back home. "We need good hospitals. We need good roads—look here at what we have," his father would say. Much of what passed for roads in those days, Ed says, were little more than ruts that were totally erased in the rainy season.

Ed's father's sermons about responsibility never quit. "Look at our land—it's overgrazed," he used to tell his son while they were out in the open country. "We've got to do something about it. And we have too many sheep—it's getting to where we have too many sheep for the people."

Ed Carlisle with his father

According to his father, education was the answer to all of the problems of the people—alcoholism, poverty, and unemployment. On his way to Church Rock, to Window Rock, to Mariano Lake, Ed Cowboy would talk and talk and talk to his boy. "We have to get our people into decent professions, and we have to get them into jobs so they can raise their families in a decent way, so that they can have their self-respect back." That idea, Ed Carlisle says, was his father's most pressing concern. "That was what it was all about—and still is: restoring our self-respect."

At least some of that self-respect, according to Ed Carlisle's story, grew from the discipline he learned at Rehoboth, and later on in the military. At Rehoboth, he says, some things were drilled into him—"Every sentence has to have a subject and a verb and a predicate," he says, smiling, as if he's still in eighth grade. "So you learned how to read and how to write."

Ed learned teamwork too—from basketball. "You learned to work together," he says. "Do your homework, don't fight with other kids, and always 'love your neighbor as yourself.'"

Today, at seventy years old, Ed Carlisle is no schoolkid; he's been out for a half century. But when he talks about what he learned at Rehoboth, he sounds as if he'd just now come from class. "In U.S. history, we learned about the Constitution and had to memorize President Abraham Lincoln's Gettysburg Address," a task he appreciates today, having visited the famous Civil War battleground.

"In literature, we did *Julius Caesar*," he says, and, without skipping a beat, he trots out most of Marc Antony's famous eulogy, as though a performance were scheduled

Ed Carlisle (far left) and basketball team

for next week: "The evil that men do lives after them, the good is oft interred with their bones."

In music, his earliest memories include children's songs like "Jesus Loves Me." But he'll never forget the hymns either, or the Negro spirituals, or classics like the "Hallelujah Chorus". "One cannot help but be moved by the words," he wrote in that memoir of his, "to be inspired with hope and compelled to worship the Lord of lords and King of kings, the Prince of Peace and Everlasting Father." He remembers lots and lots of singing during his school days, including the harmonies of Dr. Louis Bos, Art Bosscher, Ed Berkompas, and Roland Kamps.

The early lessons he learned from hours and hours of Sunday school are still there—"We are our brother's keeper," he says, and he'll never forget that cold and windy March Sunday night when Reverend Peter Eldersveld, the Christian Reformed radio minister, taught the kids all about love—the "Beauty Way" of the Christian believer—from 1 Corinthians 13.

Not all the great lessons Ed learned came from the classroom. Way back in the fourth grade, says Ed, he and all the other kids were taught how to make belts—"beautiful belts," he says, "and other artistic things that sold quickly." Some kids were overjoyed at the chance to learn these skills—Navajo arts are a storied part of reservation life, and artisans of all kinds—silversmiths and weavers— were and still are highly regarded.

"I was raised on a farm, and while I was familiar with farm and livestock work, I didn't know a thing about art," Ed says, so he was reassigned to doing janitor work for Jacob Bosscher, the superintendent of the mission compound. Bosscher was a matter-of-fact boss—he'd tell little Ed what needed to be done and how to get it done, and then he'd let him be.

Working alongside Mr. Bosscher, by way of his teaching and his example, Ed says he learned how to negotiate prices with the locals—other Navajos—who brought in meat and other supplies. "Mr. Bosscher said that the way to succeed is to treat people fairly, to be friendly—that's the way to get what you want," Ed remembers. "That will come only with mutual respect."

Those lessons—both inside and outside the classroom—were not easily forgotten, Ed says. "At Rehoboth, teaching was for life, and it came from all the folks there, faculty and staff, and within all classroom subjects," he writes in his memoir. Once again, he leans on the Word: In preparing his disciples, Jesus provided on-the-job training by example, giving them the Lord's Prayer as a model. When he sent the disciples out on the Great Commission, he told them that they would be ridiculed, hated, and suffer many trials and tribulations—even be killed. He taught them to pray for whatever they needed, "and your gracious and merciful heavenly Father is willing and able to give what you need, if you pray in my name."

That reliance on Scripture is part of Ed's complex answer to the question of "What did you learn at Rehoboth?" Years later, when he went through what he calls his "tribula-

tions" at the University of New Mexico and in the military, Ed would think back to what he had learned at Rehoboth. "Every Sunday morning Pastor Abel Poel would read the Ten Commandments," Ed recalls, "and then he'd say we should love God above all, and the second commandment is to love your neighbor as yourself." Every Sunday he heard it. And that teaching never disappeared from Ed's mind, heart, and soul.

Lifelong Learning

A certain expansiveness of spirit, of wanting to learn, of taking up opportunities— those are attributes Ed's strong education gave him as well. "Throughout my career in law, I received valuable administrative and management training because, as the junior member of whatever organization I was in, I was often sent all over the country for advanced training." Such opportunities almost always offered far more than what was advertised.

Others didn't want to go. They were tied too closely to friends and kin and the reservation, and sometimes they were simply afraid to "rub elbows with non-Indians." Because he didn't stay home, Ed met other Native people, "including the Athabascans, our relatives from Alaska, as well as thoughtful professionals from Africa, Asia, India, and other countries." Even informally, he began to recognize "common problems, as well as similar beliefs and teachings. I learned that I could communicate with my other relatives in the Athabascan-Navajo language . . . that we have similar beliefs with many Africans and Orientals. For example, we bless one another when we meet anyone. In Navajo we say, *yá'át'ééh*, which translates to mean, 'May everything under the heavens be with you.'" He sounds much like Hosteen Cowboy might have, seated under a tree to escape the hot New Mexico sun, with Andrew Vander Wagen beside him. "To me," Ed says, "that blessing reflects the essence of living the 'Beauty Way.'"

Dorothy Carlisle was Dorothy Bowman when Ed first met her in high school. Her father, a truck driver for a grocery wholesaler, was reared in the traditional way, but eventually became a Christian believer. Her uncle, Alfred Bowman, was an interpreter at the Tohatchi church. It's fair to say that Dorothy Bowman Carlisle is a "cradle Christian." Ed writes, "My wife's parents both graduated from Albuquerque Indian School. Her father was a United States Marine, a veteran of World War II, a Navajo Code Talker. Dorothy's father maintained a Christian home for their children and taught them to learn and to work hard consistently. He allowed them to choose their own professions."

As with other matriarchal Navajo families, it was Dorothy's mother who determined that her children would attend the mission school at Rehoboth. Christianity had first come into her mother's life when she was

REHOBOTH YEARBOOK

Dorothy Bowman

a boarding school student at Crownpoint. When the opportunity arose for her children to go to Rehoboth, she pushed. Dorothy attended grade school at Tohatchi, where her mother was matron, but once she graduated, she went off to Rehoboth High School, just like her two older brothers.

CHAPTER 4

Those Who Couldn't Stay Away

Jacob and Isabel Kamps and Sons

I n the 1920s, China was madly unstable. Chiang Kai-shek was on a mission to consolidate the country's many warring fiefdoms. The world communist revolution had begun to take root, gathering strength and adherents. Yet among many North American Protestant Christians, the call to minister in China was muted. The effects of World War I had not yet settled into history, and the enthusiasm some believers had felt for bringing the Word to "the heathen" was waning. Pearl S. Buck, the Nobel Prize winner for *The Good Earth*, herself a missionary to China, quite publically criticized traditional Christian missionary efforts.

In rural Michigan, a young couple might well have been oblivious to all of this. But in their enthusiasm for world missions, Jacob and Isabel Kamps had few equals. Both graduates of Hope College, both teachers by profession, the two of them met and between them arose an intense desire to bring the Word of God to the world—especially to China.

Back then, the Christian Reformed Church, a tiny Dutch transplant denomination barely

Jacob and Isabel Kamps

CALVIN COLLEGE ARCHIVES

fifty years old, was only partially acclimated to its new North American soil and had been quite content to find its own way in a culture it only vaguely understood. In the CRC, the mission enterprise was flourishing, which may help to explain Jacob and Isabel Kamps's deep dedication to the call they'd received.

They'd intended to go to China, but that wasn't where they ended up. The potential violence there made that mission impossible. So they went instead to a still-young mission field in McKinley County, New Mexico, a field that spread itself widely over the far-reaching desert landscape of the Navajo Indian Reservation and the Zuni pueblo.

That the Kamps family—sons Roland, Jack, and Phil, and even brother Gordon for extended periods of his life—still live in Gallup, New Mexico, is, some might say, happenstance. Jacob and Isabel never intended to put down roots in the American Southwest.

Home in New Mexico

Jacob Kamps's World War I military experience had created an enthusiasm for mission work. While he was serving with the armed forces, he saw a world drastically different from his family's 40-acre farm just outside the village of Drenthe, Michigan.

Then there was a turning point at a Youth for Christ event that prompted young Jacob to reset his professional goal to the ministry in general, and missions in particular. In 1926, he and Isabel, recently married, spent six months in China, training for a position in a field that would never open. Soon enough, they left the compound where they, like other North Americans, were being held for their safety. They boarded the U.S. Navy gunship *Panay* and traveled down the Yangtze to Shanghai, where they waited in an international compound for a regular steamship home. Isabel was pregnant with their oldest, Roland.

"Look," the Mission Board told the Kamps, "we've got an opening in New Mexico right now. Why don't you put in a year there until things cool off in China—and then we'll

Jacob Kamps on a visit

send you back." They never figured on staying, never guessed they would. China remained their dream.

Within a year of their arrival in Gallup, William Mierop, the official Rehoboth pastor, passed away, and Jacob Kamps was moved into that position. Early missionaries to the area were anything but specialized; they led worship wherever needed, visited families on the reservation, taught religion classes at Bureau of Indian Affairs schools, and fulfilled any number of bedside duties in the mission hospital.

Tohlakai, Mariano Lake, Mexican Springs—Jacob used to visit all over to teach religion classes. Jack remembers going along as a boy, hanging out at the trading post with a bottle of soda, sitting on the rugs while his father held forth in front of dozens of Native kids. At boarding schools, even in the Bureau of Indian Affairs schools, the law of the land demanded that Native American kids listen to some kind of religious training.

The system was arranged for the purpose of Native American assimilation into the larger culture. Native kids were expected to accept the Christian religion and give up their own.

Jack remembers hearing his father up in the study—his interpreter repeating a sentence in Navajo two and three times, and then his father repeating it time after time after time, trying to get it right. Rev. Kamps worked hard at speaking the Navajo language, and like that of Andrew Vander Wagen before him, his ministry was enriched greatly by his ability to speak with those to whom he offered the Christian gospel.

Roland is quick to add that all those hours of language training, listening over and over again to the complex pronunciations of the Navajo language from trusted and beloved interpreters ("among the wisest

men I've ever known—and I'm a teacher," Roland insists), all that language training, something Rev. Jacob Kamps took on of his own volition, gave his father an incalculably valuable understanding of the world of the people he'd come to serve. "He knew the language," Roland says, as though that answer puts to rest a host of questions. "He worked hard to learn it, and he did—many others never could or never did."

Jack also remembers his father going from camp to camp, from community to community, often picking people up on the way to church, then bringing them back on his way to the next congregation. When the van was full, Jack remembers straddling a headlight out front, as through he were scouting the road ahead, his father at the wheel, kids hanging out all the windows. It was great fun. If there was rain, some churches would

Dr. Lee Huizenga encounters New Mexico mud.

have to wait a week, because the roads became impassable.

Roland remembers the time word got home that his father wouldn't be returning that night because rain had made a mudbath of the dirt roads. Paved roads were the exception back then, and when rains came they normally came in spades, turning dusty sand into sticky, unruly red mud impossible for cars to drive through.

But then, surprisingly, Reverend Kamps showed up early the next morning. Roland Kamps still shakes his head when he puts the story together. Once the temperature dropped below freezing, Jacob and his interpreter jacked up the car, one corner at a time, took off the wheels one at a time, hacked the frozen clay off each tire, put the wheels back on, and, in the dark of night, drove off, returning home hours before they were expected. That was the life of a reservation preacher, Roland says, with clear admiration.

Missionary Kids

At many Christian colleges today, the designation "MK" identifies a particular kind of student: one who has come from a missionary family—a "missionary kid." Often such a designation arises because MKs are perceived as "something other" than a traditional student, largely because they seem so deeply cross-cultural. Sometimes it's a burden being an MK, because it may be difficult for a missionary kid to recognize just exactly where his home is.

But the Kamps boys never had that problem, it seems. All of them call Rehoboth home. Three of them have extended the

The Kamps brothers (from left to right: Phil, Jack, Gord, Lloyd, Edwin, Roland)

roots their parents gave them when they came here, and a fourth returns regularly because he can't stay away.

Why? The boys have thought about that because they recognize their uniqueness; they recognize that the vast majority of the missionary kids they knew growing up at Rehoboth have long since put down roots elsewhere. What was it about their upbringing here that was different?

Jack claims that he doesn't remember his parents ever talking as though they had missed out on something. "My parents never thought of us as suffering here, as if carrying some kind of burden as missionaries. I've heard so many missionaries talk about all of the things they gave up to be here."

What the Kamps boys remember from those early days is worth a book. They lived on the mission compound, so Rehoboth and all of its surrounding acreage was their home, their "stomping grounds." It's not all that difficult to imagine six boys let loose on hundreds of acres of open country. To them, it seemed almost Edenic.

Maybe that's why three of them never really left. Two, Jack and Phil, became physicians, and even though neither of them ever intended to return to McKinley County, New Mexico, both of them created long and successful medical practices in the neighborhood of their boyhoods. Aside from a short stint in California, Roland spent most of his professional life teaching either at Rehoboth school itself or at local public schools. During his time there, he did everything—including coaching most major sports and teaching dozens of different classes, some of which were new to him when he first opened the book. For a time, he was principal and administrator. For the old-timers

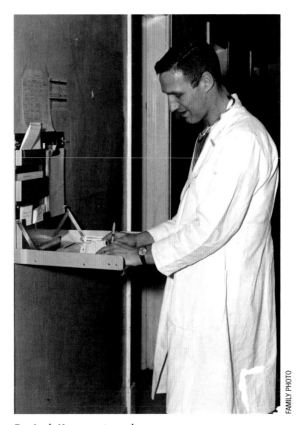

FAMILY PHOTO

Dr. Jack Kamps at work

at Rehoboth, Roland Kamps is very much a legend.

Brother Gordon held teaching and administrative positions in Christian schools from New Jersey to Montana, including a stint at Rehoboth. Retired, he still spends some time annually at Zuni, helping out at the school. Brother Ed, also retired, lives in Denver. Brother Lloyd, who lived in Chicago for much of his life, recently passed away. But the three who still live here insist that even though life itself had temporarily led them away from the Red Rocks, they always thought of Gallup—and the Rehoboth community—as home.

Jack never intended to come back—in fact, he claims that Gallup/Rehoboth was just about the last place on his list of possibilities when he and his wife, Kyse, started

Roland Kamps

hunting for a place to live and work. They wanted something somewhere between New Mexico (home for Jack) and Washington (home for Kyse).

But Dr. Avery Vanden Bosch, then the head of the Rehoboth hospital, knew how to exert pressure. "You need to come to Rehoboth," he told Jack. "You need to come back because that's your home."

But Jack declined. Then Vanden Bosch asked him whether, instead of returning, Jack would take over Vanden Bosch's own spot in a Denver practice, allowing Vanden Bosch another year at Rehoboth. Seemed like a good deal, Jack said, so he and Kyse went to Denver to put down roots.

A year later, Vanden Bosch called again— "Come and work with me," he said, which was a slightly different proposition than he'd attempted the year before. The sort of partnership Vanden Bosch was offering at

Rehoboth was worth investigating, so Jack went back to New Mexico.

"What drew me back, pure and simple, was need," he says. That the Rehoboth hospital needed young doctors was something he'd known for as long as he'd lived around the mission compound. What he'd never really understood was the need in the entire region. "The state of medical care in the whole county wasn't good," he says. Kyse admits that she was reluctant, but she agreed when Jack said it would only be for a year. "Once we were here," she says, smiling a bit, "I knew we weren't leaving."

Roland, the eldest of the brothers, attended Calvin College, but his education was interrupted by the war. He spent some time in the South Pacific after being drafted in 1944, but then, as he likes to say, "Hitler decided to quit once he knew I was in." His fourteen months of service garnered him just enough GI Bill to return and complete his education at Calvin in 1949.

He turned down a teaching job in Wisconsin that year, in part because New Mexico, with or without a job, was just too strong a pull. When he tries to explain that attraction, he becomes a Calvinist theologian: "I've always believed that God guides us with his hand and that, regardless of our intent, his purposes will be fulfilled."

Even his marriage had the Lord's designs all over it. He met his wife, Ruth, his senior year, and started dating late; in fact, she was just a freshman at Calvin. But something just clicked, unlocking a future neither of them could have foreseen. "He would never have met me if it wouldn't have been for the war," Ruth says, referring to Roland's just-sufficient GI Bill funds, "and I wouldn't have been interested if my sister hadn't been in Rehoboth." Of course, almost sixty years later, all of that theology makes undeniable sense.

Mom Kamps

But what about Isabel Kamps, the woman who was bound and determined to preach the gospel in China? To the boys, she was as remarkable as her husband.

Her sons say that in all those years living close to the reservation she never turned away a stranger from her door. When someone asked her whether, with six boys, she hadn't missed having a daughter, she responded that one can't really miss what one never had.

She graduated as valedictorian from Hudsonville (Michigan) High School somewhere around 1917, and then again from Hope College, just a few years later, in a time when few women ever attended school be-

yond the eighth grade. She was brilliant and devoted.

She was a missionary, but her boys claim she never considered her life a *mission*, as in "something from which one returns." Her life was mission in the broadest sense: an eternal calling. Her boys insist that neither she nor her husband ever once considered their life on the edge of the reservation to be a burden.

For years, some of the missionaries and staff and medical people from Rehoboth climbed "the pyramid" in the Red Rocks just to the north, and Isabel always went along, every Memorial Day. The last time she hiked up there for a sunrise breakfast she was eighty-plus years old.

You may want to imagine her as the mother of six rambunctious boys, knee-deep in rattlesnake country. But you need a picture of a woman named Isabel Kamps—

Army doctor Phil Kamps

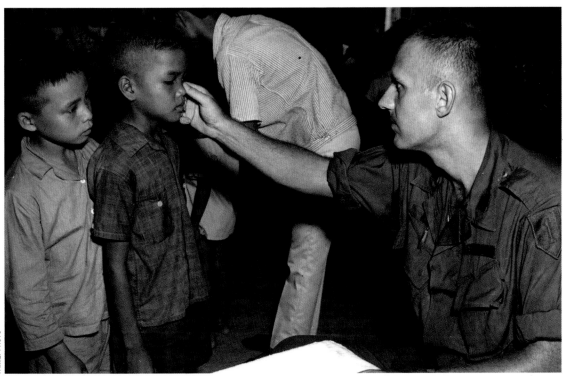

Jack, Roland, and Phil Kamps today.

twice valedictorian—way up there on the dome of Red Rock, a piece of homemade muffin in hand, the incandescent New Mexico sun pulling color from a broad expanse of breathtaking creation all around, a prayer on her lips and her eyes wide open to what she undoubtedly would have seen as God's glorious creation.

That was Isabel Kamps.

Just Give Us Sand

In 1941-42, while Dad stayed behind and ministered to an outlying church that was vacant, working hard on Navajo language studies, the rest of the family—Mom and five of the boys—spent a year in Michigan, in part because it just seemed prudent eco-nomically. There was no way the Reverend Kamps and his wife could pay for room and board and tuition for all those students, two of them at Calvin College. So the college kids lived with Isabel in a Grand Rapids house while the three other boys also attended Christian schools.

One day, the youngest, Phil, was obviously bored, as were the other boys. "We didn't enjoy ourselves all that much [in Grand Rapids]," Jack says. "I was in eighth, and Phil was in fourth." Their mother was trying hard to mount some enthusiasm and rid the air of homesickness—after all, she'd been born and reared in West Michigan. "You've got all this green—you've got all this green to play in," she repeated, pointing at the wonderful lawn outside the front window. "Just look all this grass."

"I hate grass," Phil said, like the kid he was.

Today the boys laugh at that one. "Just give us sand—you know?" Jack says.

"You can do things with sand," Phil adds, "but you can't do a thing with grass. Here in New Mexico, we had the whole outdoors."

It wasn't always easy. A couple of them were the only white kids in their classes, and being the only one of anything is never all that easy. Rehoboth, then and now, was never Eden, really. Besides, the Kamps boys know bad stories as well as good ones. They weren't sinless themselves—just ask them and they'll narrate some hair-raising hijinks.

But to them, New Mexico was home. And it still is, as it is for many of their kids and grandkids.

Home is where the heart is—the place to which you are called.

When marauding warlords shut down the Chinese mission field, Rev. Jacob Kamps and his wife Isabel were deeply and powerfully saddened. China had been their dream.

But they went, willingly, to a place they didn't know much about—a new mission field on the reservation in the New Mexico desert, even if it was only for a year. Turned out to be a lifetime.

Here at Rehoboth, they bloomed in the red desert soil where they were planted—as have their children. "Returning to this community was the Lord's leading," Jack says, "He has blessed us here."

That he has.

CHAPTER 5

The Spiral Staircase

Ted and Evelyn Charles

J ust inside the door of Ted and Evelyn Charles's two-story log hogan is a studio full of drawings and photographs, brushes and pens, rocks and stones. Ted Charles is a craftsman and an artist by predilection and practice. Stones are his latest interest. But to call what he does with them a "craft" sells his commitments short. Lately, he's been making arrowheads cut from stones. But he's making neither war nor money with what he fashions. Instead, he's trying to gain a foothold in his own heritage by sculpting the flint and obsidian in the very same manner his ancestors did.

When Ted was a boy, his grandfather created a bow in the old-fashioned way and gave it to Ted. It was a gift he didn't fully appreciate until years later, when his own Navajo heritage started to carry meaning. That bow disappeared with his childhood, but the stones and sinew and fletching strewn over his studio are the particulars of a quest to value what's been lost.

"We're talking about a people who knew their environment well enough to locate everything they needed," says Ted. "Grandfa-

Ted and Evelyn Charles

ther must have learned what he knew from his father and uncles, a long time ago." That craftsmanship has been left behind— tragically so, he believes. So he's trying to make a bow and arrows as his grandfather might have—the old way, the traditional way. He does this not because he's into antiques but because he wants to understand what those ancestors knew and how they lived, lest all that knowledge and history be lost forever.

That quest also explains the two-story hogan high on a hill amid junipers and pinions. The Charles's home sits atop a settlement of homes just off I-40 near Cibola National Forest, a gorgeous place for a gorgeous home. When Ted's aging parents needed their help, Ted and Evelyn Charles sold their house in Gallup, as well as parents' house, and built the home they designed—the world's only two-story hogan, as they like to say, smiling.

An Immense Loss

There's another reason the two-story hogan stands on that particular hill, and that reason is perfectly understandable to every tribe and nation, and especially to every parent.

Early on the morning of October 7, 1988, the Charles family left Gallup in two cars to celebrate Evelyn's parents' fiftieth wedding anniversary in Denver. Sons David and Mark were riding together. In Albuquerque, a few hours east, the whole family stopped for breakfast. David said an opening prayer. After they left the diner, the two cars were separated. But the family had agreed that they would meet at the rest stop at Raton Pass, 100 miles northeast of Santa Fe.

A few hours later, Mom and Dad and the girls—Denise, Millie, and Linda—sat waiting at Raton Pass. They waited. And waited. No sign of the boys. Finally, they tacked a note on the rest stop's bulletin board and went on, bewildered.

When they arrived in Denver, Evelyn called home and spoke to the woman who was caring for Ted's aging mother. She told them harrowing news: the state police were looking for them because David and Mark had been in an accident south of Santa Fe.

"The world turned upside down," Evelyn says.

They called the Santa Fe hospital and talked to a doctor. He told them that Mark had sustained a head injury and could explain nothing about the accident. He was badly hurt but in stable condition. The doctor needed a parental signature to operate.

"And our other son?" Ted asked.

The doctor said, "That was *your* son?" And then he spoke the words that are seared into Ted and Evelyn's memories: "Dead on arrival." The doctor hadn't known that both boys were theirs.

What happened next—the body, the funeral, the grief—is not a blur. Ted and Evelyn can still walk you through those agonizing days as though all the horror transpired only yesterday. But one of the means by which they have learned to deal with the immense loss of their oldest boy—a sweet and kind track star at Rehoboth High School, a responsible and considerate son who'd just graduated from tech school—is the two-story hogan.

"It was meant to be a memorial for David in an attempt to reach toward heaven," Evelyn says. Way up there on top of a hill, high above the mesas and red rocks, their home is also a memorial pledge to meet their son someday on high. They want the place to be a retreat center—a place for renewal, a place to meditate and praise the Lord.

Ted says that through those next months and years he held his grief with the gritty stoicism of the Marine he was once trained to be. But for a while, every Friday at ten, about the moment David was killed, he'd stand speechless in front of his classroom, frozen in time.

Evelyn—mom—was no ex-Marine. Difficult questions flooded her mind and heart and soul. Journaling helped her deal with the grief, she says. In an article she wrote for *The Banner* (Sept. 30, 1991), she remembered especially their trip to David's gravesite in the Rehoboth cemetery on the first anniversary of his death.

The cemetery was noisy that day as the raucous cheers of high school kids carried across the open land from a track meet. "We stood by our truck," she wrote in that article, "which had David's headstone in the back, and waited for the race to finish. We could hear the crowd cheering as the runners came over the finish line, and we remembered all the times we had stood at the sidelines cheering David on. We wept openly because all we had now was a headstone in the back of the truck.

"We often feel that we're climbing a spiral staircase on which we are passing the same areas of pain over and over again," she admitted in that essay, almost twenty years ago now. Much has changed, but the hurt is still there on the spiral staircase.

To say that something good grew from David's death is both fanciful and unfair to the suffering that Ted and Evelyn and their children went through. No one can gloss over their agony. "No, we aren't getting over it," Evelyn wrote in that *Banner* piece.

But both of them agree that something happened in those next weeks and months that, over time, made life easier. Something brought them back, not so much to faith itself—Ted was preaching in local churches at the time—but to a source of rich strength they'd missed for a while: a loving community. Rehoboth helped to restore them with its love, its care, its vigilant grace in their lives.

A Missionary Nurse

Ted and Evelyn Charles come from very different backgrounds, and while they met at Rehoboth, they haven't always been in love with the place.

Evelyn Natelborg is not Navajo, nor Zuni. Evelyn Natelborg is as wholly Dutch-American as her husband is Navajo. Theirs is what people used to call a "mixed marriage," one of many through the years in Rehoboth mission history.

Evelyn came to Rehoboth after studying in Grand Rapids, Michigan, at Reformed Bible College and working at Blodgett Hospital. She had long ago made a commitment to medical missions.

"I'd lived a very sheltered life," she'll tell you. "I'd gone to Christian schools, Calvin College, and Reformed Bible College, and I hadn't been outside the Christian Reformed Church at all." She explains herself in a way that shows she's spent a lot of time trying to understand her own motivations. That confidence makes her story convincing.

She says she didn't really want to go to Africa, and that she wasn't even all that thrilled to go to New Mexico in 1964. Her motivation, she says, was quite simple: "I thought God wouldn't love me if I didn't do something special for him." So, newly capped as a nurse, she signed on the dotted line to work at Rehoboth Christian Hospital. She came to McKinley County, New Mexico, a place some people call the "Indian Capital of America," thinking primarily of things above, not here below.

She was young; most of the hospital staff were far older. She hadn't intended to make medical missions in New Mexico a long-term commitment. But her peers at the hospital were lifelong missionary nurses. She was accustomed to an ordinary eight-hour workday, but at Rehoboth she was awarded marathon shifts. She had been taught specialization; but at Rehoboth she worked everything from pediatrics to the mop and pail, often cleaning up blood. Some nights she was the only staff member in the hospital, the only person there to open the door when new patients arrived. She hadn't imagined herself doing any of that.

Evelyn didn't want to tell the other nurses how downhearted she felt, because they saw their calling as irreversible. Some afternoons she would get off work late and hike up to the hill east of the campus, then climb a tree and sing old hymns:

> Why should I feel discouraged, why
>   should the shadows come,
> Why should my heart be lonely, and
>   long for heaven and home,
> When Jesus is my portion? My con-
>   stant friend is He:
> His eye is on the sparrow, and I
>   know He watches me;
> His eye is on the sparrow, and I
>   know He watches me.

It's unlikely that Evelyn Natelborg would have said it then, but she will tell you today that back then God Almighty didn't seem to be watching her at all. She felt far outside the orbit of God's love, in part because she couldn't generate the unfaltering commitment of the older nurses. She was young and alone, and now, having arrived at the setting where she thought God had called her, that very divine love and care that she wanted so badly seemed nowhere to be found. She was a medical missionary, so why wasn't she happy? Nothing made sense.

So when ex-Marine Ted Charles asked her for a date, she had no idea what to do. Was it proper for a white girl on the hospital staff to date a Navajo man? Was that

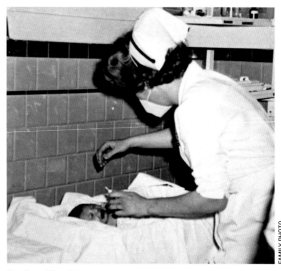

Evelyn Charles

what God wanted? Even though as a nurse she served the Navajo and Zuni people of the region, she admits today that she knew very little about them. She was serving sick men, women, and children she didn't know or understand. And now one of them had asked her for a date.

A Navajo Missionary Kid

Who was this Ted Charles, and what had brought him back to Rehoboth?

If you ask Ted that question, he might well answer this way: "My name is Ted Charles. I am the son of John and Mae Charles. I was born into the Water Flows Together Clan of the Bitter Water people. My *che* on my mother's side, the Black Street Wood People clan, and the Bear Enemy clan on my grandfather's side." But back then, Ted wasn't so sure of his roots.

Evelyn might well begin her family story with immigration—the time her own forbears left the Netherlands for a new world blossoming with opportunity. Ted, like many Navajos, begins his story with a radically different narrative. He starts with "the Long Walk." He starts with the time when

Col. Kit Carson and U.S. troops began a merciless military campaign that destroyed crops and livestock, burned villages, and killed the *Dineh*, the Navajos, in order to carry out government policy—the relocation of an entire people. Thousands of Navajos left their homeland to walk to Fort Sumner, 300 miles away. Along the way, hundreds perished in the cold.

Ted's maternal grandfather survived the Long Walk when he was just a boy. When his people returned to their ancestral land, he settled near Mariano Lake. Ted's mother was born in 1919, in a hogan, one of 19 children in a family of sheepherders and horse traders. Mae C. Casemero was, Ted says, a tiny woman with a huge heart and an instinctive penchant for horses.

She was also the first in the family to listen closely to the gospel of Jesus Christ, the good news she heard while she was a student at a boarding school at Crownpoint, where the CRC had a ministry to the boarding students.

Ted's father's family was abusive, so his father was taken from that home and enrolled at the Ft. Lewis BIA boarding school in Colorado. There he was given the Anglo name of John Morgan Charles. A few years later he was sent to the Methodist mission school at Farmington, where he did well in athletics and academics, so well that he continued his education at Haskell Indian Training School in Kansas and Simpson College in Iowa. When the Depression hit, John Morgan Charles returned to the reservation, where he took a job with the Bureau of Indian Affairs at Crownpoint. That's where he met Mae Casemero.

According to Ted, his mother's introduction to Christianity did not lead initially to a deep commitment. Both his mother and father were traditionally bound to their families. Ted, their second child, came along in 1941 after the family had moved to Mexican Springs, one of a series of moves that put them in Shiprock for eight years of Ted's boyhood. It was there, in an independent church led by Rehoboth graduate J. C. Morgan, that the family began attending worship regularly.

When Morgan left to become Chairman of the Navajo Nation, the Charles family began to worship at the Shiprock CRC. There they learned the catechism, were baptized, and made profession of faith, guided by Rev. Floris Vander Stoep.

John Charles, as highly educated as anyone on the northern reaches of the reservation in those years, wanted the best schools for his children. So he moved his family once again, to Farmington. Ted, one of just a few Navajo kids there, attended the public school. Going to a public school, he says, shaped him deeply: "I went to school most of my life with Anglo kids," he says, "so I knew how to talk to Anglos, knew how to associate with them, even took piano lessons."

When Ted was thirteen, his father became a translator for Rev. George Yff and moved the family once again, this time to Rehoboth itself, where Ted was enrolled in the ninth grade.

Rehoboth

Not all of Ted's memories of Rehoboth in those years are pleasant—and for good sociological reasons. Throughout his teenage years, when finding one's place is difficult for anyone, at Rehoboth Ted Charles was "neither fish nor fowl."

Unlike most of the Native kids, Ted lived with his family right there on the compound,

Winter at Rehoboth in the 1920s

and not in the dorms. Because of his earlier education in the public school in Farmington, he had more confidence around Anglo kids than did other Navajo boys, and that confidence set him apart from the reservation kids. His father thought the Navajo language was best abandoned in the new world the Navajo people faced, so he wouldn't speak it at home.

But Ted Charles was not an Anglo either. Anglos were treated in a different way than Native kids, and that confused him. White boys had their own dorms and their own rules: they didn't have to get up early for study halls and could go home on weekends. What's more, with his parents out spreading the gospel into every corner of the region, and no garden to tend (as in previous backyards), Ted says he had far too much free time.

When he graduated from high school, his father pushed him to go to Dordt College in Iowa, instead of to New Mexico State, where he'd already applied and received a scholarship. He respected his father's judgment, he says, so he took a bus to Iowa with no idea what he was getting into.

There was another Native American student at Dordt at that time, a Winnebago. The two of them would sometimes talk about what they were feeling in the Anglo world, the Dutch world, in which they'd suddenly found themselves. When his friend quit school, Ted was more confused than he'd ever been about who he was.

He'd never made profession of faith, even though it had been urged on him. But the kids he knew at Dordt College, as much as he liked them, didn't seem all that pious to him, all that given to walking the straight-

and-narrow. Ted still struggled to determine who he was. So he left.

The Marine Corps

In 1962, just a year later, Ted and hundreds of other Marines could see Cuba from the deck of their ship. The whole company waited to be told when to climb down the nets into the landing boats for a battle from which, they were warned, few of them would return. "I would have been front line," he remembers. "We could see the land, the beach, and in your mind you can visualize where those gun placements were, and all the time you're thinking that it's not going to be me—it's going to be the other guy."

The Marines were closely watching the status of a Russian trawler carrying missiles, the trawler everyone in America was also watching at that very hour. "If that ship didn't turn around," Ted says, "we were instructed to blow it out of the water, our cue to get on shore." They knew this was something big. Battleships were backing them up, canons pointing toward land. Then the trawler turned around, never entering the harbor. The Cuban Missile Crisis was over.

Oddly enough, it was the military that sparked Ted's interest in and commitment to his Native roots. Part of it was the whole idea of being a warrior, a cultural role far more significant among Native people than

Ted Charles (center) with fellow Marines

among Anglos. Warriors stand at the top of the social scale in tribal life, but not simply because of their ability to fight. "As a warrior, you don't only give protection to others," he says, "but you're also obligated to be of a generous nature to those who are in need. Those who are poor and cannot hunt—*you* provide for them. That's the old traditional way." A Native warrior is not just a leader in war, but also a leader in peace.

That's what Ted talked about with his buddies: an Ojibwa from Minnesota, a Comanche from Oklahoma, a Blackfoot from Montana. In training at Camp Pendleton, they'd hung out together, often at the ocean when they could get a precious few hours off. "We'd go down to San Clemente, where we'd make a makeshift coffee-can drum and sing away. We would teach each other certain songs, then all join in. Someone would know a powwow song, and we'd sing others that had tribal significance. That's when I began to make a sense of my identity, of who I am."

And it wasn't just their history that brought them together; all three had had similar experiences in education. One of them hated everything having to do with Christianity because of the way he'd been mistreated in mission schools. In the military—perhaps the least segregated institution of society at that time—Ted Charles began to search for some part of his heritage.

A New Relationship

After his stint in the Marines was over and Ted returned home to Rehoboth, he was different because he'd come to understand something about *difference*. He was offered a job as a dorm aide, and he took it. And that's where he first spotted Evelyn Natelborg, one of the new nurses the guys on

Ted and Evelyn Charles on their wedding day

staff eyed closely when they walked into the dining hall early that year.

By the time Ted got up his courage and sauntered over, he wasn't an unknown. Evelyn had met his grandmother when she was a patient in the hospital. What's more, she knew Ted's parents.

"From Denver, eh?" the ex-Marine said to her. "So what brings you out here?"

That wasn't a question she would have answered for just anyone, homesick and bewildered as she was. "Got an hour?" she said.

"Sure—how about Sunday night?" Ted said. And that's how it started.

Evelyn remembers that very first date—a church date—an evening service in town. After it was over, Ted ran into a Navajo couple and the three joked around in their own way, a way Evelyn didn't understand. She says she felt as though she'd come from another planet.

And it wasn't easy to date back then at Rehoboth. Sometimes, outside the boys' dorm, the two of them would talk late into the night, oblivious to the wide-eyed kids behind open windows straining to hear every word.

When things between them started to get serious, Evelyn called her mother. "Guess who's coming to dinner?" she said. Her parents accepted that she was dating a Native boy, as long as he was a Christian. But her mother wondered, rather shyly, how dark-skinned Ted was. Evelyn compared him to a kid they knew in Denver. But there was no bitterness, no animosity, on her parents' part. Not long after, Ted and Evelyn were engaged.

Ted wanted to return to school to get a degree in physical education and start a career as a teacher. So he applied to Biola College in California, was accepted, and enrolled. The next summer they were married, and they left Rehoboth for Los Angeles.

Separation

Rehoboth had an opening when Ted graduated, so he, Evelyn, and their young son David went back home to New Mexico. "To teach at Rehoboth in those days," Ted remembers, "you had to be a jack-of-all-trades, master of none." Bible, typing, PE, catechism on Sunday afternoons for boarding school kids, Wednesday night religion instruction classes for the kids at Wingate High—teaching was much more than a full-time job. Coaching meant year-round practices and hundreds of miles of travel back and forth to rival schools.

The mid-1970s were a difficult time in Native American life. Just about every reservation had its own chapter of the American Indian Movement (AIM). Black Power and Gay Power and Feminist Power birthed Red Power. But militancy and nativism among Native people made white folks uneasy. Standoffs at Wounded Knee and Alcatraz created banner headlines. Downtown Gallup turned hot and angry; the mayor was taken hostage. At Rehoboth some students donned jackets with "AIM" printed on the back.

At Native mission schools all over the West, significant change was taking place. Relationships between the races became testy, then angry, as Native people began, more than they had for years, to look back for an identity more and more of them understood to have been abusively ripped away.

It was not an easy time for the Charles family, either. The job at Rehoboth required that Ted be apart from the needs of a growing family. "I remember times when he would leave at six on Saturday morning and get back at ten that night," Evelyn says.

So Evelyn was often home alone with their three kids and two foster kids. She was also working in the clinic from eight to five. Life was stressful. Folks from the villages just southeast of Rehoboth recognized which house in the mission compound was home to other Navajos. People often showed up at their door, looking for help, asking for handouts.

In 1977, after seven years at Rehoboth, the pressures to fit what both of them saw as a certain Rehoboth mold just got to be too much—and Ted resigned.

Leaving Rehoboth was terribly hard on both of them. But to Evelyn, pulling out meant leaving the only verifiably safe neighborhood she knew of in McKinley County. At Rehoboth, kids rode all over on their bikes, climbed trees, and hiked through

Ted Charles at his easel

the surrounding hills, fearing nothing. Home was a precious neighborhood of friends. Even though she knew they needed to leave, it seemed as if they were being tossed from the Garden.

Most marriages, at one time or another, become imperiled. When Ted and Evelyn Charles were forced to move into Gallup from the village of Rehoboth, both of them wondered, for a time anyway, whether their marriage could ride out the storm. A range of emotions flooded them—sadness, fear, rejection, bewilderment—and resentment toward Rehoboth festered as they sought to find their place in the world without the support of the Rehoboth community that had brought them together.

For two years Ted worked in a downtown Gallup jewelry store. They found a house on the west side of the city. But Ted was a teacher. He loved kids, and he loved teaching. Those years were the toughest, and for many reasons.

Sometimes Ted and Evelyn felt rejected by Rehoboth, and when you feel rejected by the family of God it's hard not to feel rejected by God himself.

Then, "out of the darkness of the night," Ted says, an old friend who was the principal of Navajo Pine told him the school there had an opening. "We need a PE teacher," he told Ted. School started in three days.

For the rest of his working life, Ted Charles taught Navajo students, at a pace that was comfortably closer to his own. For the rest of his working life, at a couple of different Navajo schools, Ted Charles taught kids in a tone and spirit that were his, not someone else's. And he prospered.

When traditional kids would tell him their grandparents believed that dissecting an earthworm was wrong, Ted could explain that just as that child's grandmother would bless a sheep before killing it, giving thanks for its sustenance, the same could be done for the earthworm—not because they would eat it but because the earthworm was giving itself for a greater purpose. Mr. Charles prospered in those schools because he knew how the kids thought and what they felt.

Reconciliation

Years after they'd left Rehoboth, the sting of what felt to them like rejection never quite went away—even though David was a great runner at Rehoboth High and Mark a star basketball player, and the girls attended there too. And then David was killed.

The funeral was at Rehoboth. High school kids came in droves. "There was really, really great support from a wider Christian community too—they were all there for us,"

Charles family members on the spirial staircase

GARY NEDERVELD

Evelyn says. "There was always good help for us through those next weeks."

Hot dishes and desserts filled the freezer because there was no more room in the fridge. Cards poured in incessantly. People called, offered their prayers, their shoulders, and their blessed silence. Old friends showed up to pray—and cry. Strong arms lifted them up, and the power of the Almighty filled them, even though the hands they felt beneath them were those of ordinary men, women, and kids. On a path no parents—or siblings—should ever have to walk alone, Ted and Evelyn Charles and their children were deeply comforted by those who willingly shared what they could of their deep sorrow.

To say that David's death is all behind them is to tell a lie. But then the house itself—that two-story hogan with the spiral staircase—bears witness.

Today, Ted and Evelyn Charles minister to the believers at Fort Wingate Christian Reformed Church, where Ted opens the Word—*and* plays the piano—every Sunday. Today, with a deer antler, Ted is learning how to sharpen arrowheads out of rock. Today, the two of them are retired, but their home is a place of community and retreat, a significant part of their ministry.

If you want to hear Ted's story, he'll tell you about Noah's sons. There were three of them, he'll tell you, and after the flood the three all departed in different directions. "My journey began when the sons of Noah dispersed in different directions from where they'd disembarked from the boat," he'll tell you joyfully. "It is my belief that I am a descendent of Shem, along the line of our Savior Jesus Christ, who was himself from the lineage of Shem. There is," he says, "that

The two-story hogan

connection between the Native American and Jewish people."

And that's a point that must be made, because many Native people who reject Christ do so because of what Jesus represents, both in their minds and in the stories of the people. To them, Jesus Christ is not the Savior of all humankind, but part of an awful story of exploitation, of the Long Walk and cultural abuse and just about everything that has gone wrong in Native life for the last 400 years. Too often Jesus Christ is seen only as the white man's god.

Ted Charles is adamant on this point: Jesus Christ belongs as much to the Navajo as to the Dutch, to the Zuni as to the Malaccan. Just read it for yourself, he'll tell you. It's right there in the first book of the Bible.

The Two-story Hogan

When Navajos speak of their land, they're not talking about limestone or red rocks, nor simply about a commodity that can be bartered or sold, but of their heritage itself.

The relationship between the *Dineh*, the people, and the *Dineteh*, the land, is deep and heartfelt. It's a spiritual bond with their beloved corner of the earth, a relationship that makes selling the land something almost unimaginable.

If you take the spiral staircase upstairs in the Charles's hogan, stand on the upper deck with Ted and Evelyn, and look out onto incredible sandstone formations twenty and thirty miles away in almost every direction, you'll know immediately that their silence bespeaks a particular kind of awe. What Ted knows in his heart—*because* he's Navajo—is that all that land is his. Not because he owns it, but because in a certain mystical way it owns *him*, and he is a part of it. Those who view property as an investment have no idea of what that means.

And yet, it was more than ethnic and racial pride or gorgeous views that made Ted and Evelyn build the hogan where and how they did. Their home is a memorial, a promise of resurrection, a reminder of an identity formed long before immigration or the Long Walk, before Noah's ark and his children's leaving. It's an eternal promise of real life somewhere in the glorious azure of the wide-brimmed desert sky. Today, they open their home to others for rest and retreat. It's a place where the beauty of creation speaks in such lovely language that those who come cannot help but be drawn to "the heart of God"—the name they use themselves to describe their retreat center.

Like the apostle Paul, Ted and Evelyn Charles will sing and preach the resurrection because what brings them great joy, even on the spiral staircase they still walk, is the promise of life itself, of reconciliation in eternity.

CHAPTER 6

Life with the Good Shepherd

Tommie and Nancy Tso

The Toyee chapel is gone now, but you'd have to see it to believe how small it was. Years ago, back in the 1930s, its adobe walls were constructed by people who wanted a place to worship the Lord. It stood there for years on a relatively nondescript piece of New Mexico reservation soil.

That church had its moments, of course, as one might expect. One of the most memorable was the time forty people crowded in for a very special worship service with Pastor Charlie Gray officiating. It was March 1987, and winter's unremitting grasp was keeping everything cold. Soon enough, the place warmed up, with the old stove stoked up to throw out heat and a friendly crowd of family and friends generating their own warm kindliness.

A celebration was going on inside—a sacrament, in fact. All five of Tommie and Nancy's Tso's kids were going to be baptized, along with their mother. Tommie had been baptized as an infant, years before.

Whether or not anyone recorded that worship service isn't clear, but Nancy Tso

Tommie and Nancy Tso

remembers. Tommie does too. That day, about a fifth of the crowd assembled was baptized in one startlingly wonderful winter afternoon.

Not long before, Nancy had come to that little chapel early one Sunday afternoon, when it was just herself and Pastor Gray. "You know," he'd said that day, before

Pastor Charlie Gray

anyone else was around, "it's a bit odd that you and Tommie send all those kids off to Rehoboth, a Christian school, but you're not even baptized yourself." And then he fixed his best pastoral look on her. "Do you want to take catechism?" he asked.

And she said yes. And so she did—she and her family with her.

He'd brought it up several times before in visits to their home. Pastor Gray was part of her clan—a particular Navajo relationship that has no direct correlative in Anglo culture. Think of it as a church small-group that meets for decades, for centuries even, so that its members trace their shared spiritual lineage back a long time. A clan is more than an extended family, but the intimacy generated between clan members finds its closest approximation in an Anglo world in the manner by which blood relatives know each other. In a sense, when they spoke together, Nancy Tso and Pastor Charlie Gray were relatives; it was as if he were a real brother, she says.

So when he'd challenged her about becoming baptized, his asking wasn't in any sense a command. It was an intimate and personal request borne from an intimate and personal relationship. What Pastor Gray had asked, in other words, couldn't be easily dismissed.

And he was right. For years—ever since she was a child, in fact—Nancy Silversmith Tso had wanted to send her children to the school at Rehoboth. She had never attended that school herself, and neither had her husband; but she'd always wanted to, and so had he. The two of them had always shared a commitment to send their children to the school at Rehoboth.

Boyhoods and Girlhoods

What hadn't been part of Tommie and Nancy's motivation was the conviction that they were children of the Lord God Almighty. Maybe their lack of conviction should be explained this way: what they knew in their heads had never quite made it convincingly into their hearts. What they knew of Rehoboth, they liked; other family members had attended, and the place had an excellent reputation.

When Rehoboth kids transferred to Wingate High School (a boarding school) back in the late 50s when Tommie and Nancy were Wingate students, those Rehoboth

Toyee Chapel

Students at Wingate High School

kids were always head-and-shoulders above the rest academically, Nancy remembers. At Wingate, star athlete Tommie had come to respect the kids he'd played against at Rehoboth—good players, good people. Even though neither had ever attended Rehoboth, both were committed to sending their kids there, even before there were any kids to enroll.

In a way, a chapter or two of Tommie Tso's family history is set right there where Rehoboth stands. He says that when his grandma was a girl, she used to herd sheep on the old Smith ranch, which eventually became the grounds of Rehoboth. Two of his aunts had attended Rehoboth in the 1920s—Rose and Bernice, daughters of Joe Capitan, who lived back then in the Toyee area. There was a connection between his family and the mission even before he was born.

Even though her sisters attended, Tommie's mother, Violet, never went to school at all, perhaps because she always loved herding the sheep her family kept. Like so many their age, both Tommie and Nancy herded sheep themselves from the time they were little. Some of that work they remember fondly: sitting atop the hills and looking

down on the sheep below. Some of it they remember not so fondly: herding sheep that veered off where they were not supposed to and wouldn't be told otherwise.

In those days, missionaries from Tohatchi CRC and even from Crownpoint CRC used to come for camp visits to Tommie's grandfather's hogan in the Toyee area. It happened often, and in those conversations the missionaries would bring up the possibility of the little kids going to school at Rehoboth.

Nancy started school at Pinedale Day School, where she also was visited by Rehoboth missionaries who would show up promptly every Wednesday afternoon to talk about Jesus and lead hymn-sings that rang out so loud people at the Trading Post just down the road would look up from their chatting, wondering if they were hearing an angelic choir.

But when it became time for Tommie to head off to school, his parents sent him to the boarding school at Crownpoint—and later to Wingate, where he met Nancy and where both of them together attended, almost weekly, Sunday religious exercises. "Some kids went to the Catholics, a few to

Keeping sheep meant having wool for weaving.

the Baptists, some to the Mormons—but the majority went to the Christian Reformed Bible instruction," Nancy remembers. First there was singing, and then all the children would be dismissed to their Sunday school classes.

At Wingate High, Tommie excelled at athletics, starting at fullback for all his three years of high school and breaking the 10-second mark in the 100-yard dash. One year younger than her husband, Nancy definitely had her eye on him in high school, but then, she says, jokingly, "Everybody wanted that star," rolling her eyes a bit after all these years.

Neither of them has ever lost the love of sports. For years, even after their own children had graduated from Rehoboth, they attended ball games, and today they're still there because their granddaughter plays on the basketball team. They insist they wouldn't miss a game—girls *or* boys.

Once Tommie graduated—a year ahead of Nancy—he headed out to technical school in Okmulgee, Oklahoma. There he started studying electronics, then switched to mechanical drafting, and graduated after two years. When he got out, like so many of his friends, he wanted to get into the service, maybe the Marines. But a problem with his wrist laid him up and kept him out. When a job opened up for a draftsman in the BIA office in Gallup, he got it.

While Tommie was in Oklahoma, Nancy started her post-secondary education in Hayward, California, where she was training as a key-punch operator. But she didn't like California much, and she missed Tommie, too. So she left California after completing her training, went back to Gallup, and showed up at the hospital where Tommie was recuperating from surgery. Was he surprised to see her? "Yes," he says weakly, a wry smile on his face, as after all these years together he's still playing hard to get. They were married a year later in January of 1964.

Tommie Tso stayed with the work he was trained for as a draftsman, even though he switched employers eventually, ending up with Navajo Tribal Utilities in Window Rock, Arizona. By that point in his life, however, he and Nancy had moved to Tohatchi after Nancy took a job at a new boarding school there. She worked as a dorm parent for twenty years on the day shift and ten years at night. All that while Tommie and Nancy were building a family—six kids, all of them eventually Rehoboth graduates.

On top of everything else, they were building their dream home. Tommie designed it, and, when they were old enough, the older kids helped build it. The site was adjacent to the home place where Tommie had grown up.

Good Shepherds

When Tommie's parents died and left the family with livestock—cattle and sheep and goats—Tommie and Nancy decided simply to move back to the home place themselves. That's where they live today.

Today with wry smiles, neither of them claims to be all that thrilled with tending livestock, but they've returned to shepherding, a job they never thought they'd see again. Both of them had long and successful professions elsewhere; both did well in those jobs. Sometimes they shake their heads when they think of it.

How large is their flock? "We've got 34 sheep," Nancy says immediately. "I just counted them this morning." To describe her tone as proud or joyous would be overstatement. That doesn't mean, however, that she doesn't like what she's doing. When Grandpa Tso died, someone had to keep

up the herd—and now their numbers have grown.

Not long ago, Tommie graciously gave his wife the opportunity to take a nap after she'd spent a day out with the sheep. He went out and did the chores himself, bringing the sheep back in. What he didn't do, Nancy says, was count well. She says she went down to the pen the next morning and determined that several were missing, then got the dogs and went out and found them.

If you listen to them talk about the livestock, it's clear that some of their bluster is a bluff. The truth is, they love having moved out to the home place, and the sheep and the cattle and the goats—they're more than just tolerable.

For Tommie and Nancy and all those who once tended sheep—and for those who still do—"the Good Shepherd" is not some odd or ancient image. It's very real. That poem reads more visually to those who've sat on

The Tso dream home

KEN KOOIMEN

67

KEN KOOIMAN

Nancy Tso with some of the family's sheep

hills and watched the flock beneath them than it does to those who don't know a sheep from a goat. "Having sheep," Nancy says, "—sometimes when you're with them and you know so well what sheep are like, then you start to think that we're like them, too, like those sheep. When they get lost and don't come back, it really worries you. You have to go and look."

All of that was very real to them as children—and still is today to two retirees who find themselves back where they started in life, looking out for God's own creatures. The idea of the Good Shepherd isn't a museum-piece at all. "That's what Jesus does to us," she says, "—and so many times too. Many times we wandered off, but I guess

Jesus saw that and he brought us back to the fold."

Back Home Again

For many years, Tommie and Nancy Tso were a success story on the reservation. Both of them had educations, both had good jobs, and together they raised a good family. There were times when the Tsos had more than their share of problems—and times when they didn't. But through many years, they say, they just didn't know the Lord. They knew *of* him, but they just didn't let him into their hearts.

Not that they hadn't heard. Nancy recounts that when her Auntie Annie Morgan used to talk to her about the Christian faith, years and years ago, in a way that she's really never

68

forgotten. Annie Morgan was a believer, and she, too, was a member of Nancy's clan. She used to take Nancy and her sisters aside and tell them in that profoundly intimate way that only clan members can that the Christian life was better than traditional ways because of this: with Christ a child lives forever. She used to say all of that in the Navajo language, of course, but before she'd start in, she'd say, *"shiyázhí."* "It means, 'my kids,' 'my child,' 'my baby,'" Nancy says. "In those terms she would tell us this new way was a better life for us." Annie Morgan told her about Jesus in a way that would never leave her.

So it was there for a long, long time—this well understood view of the Christian gospel. It just took the Good Shepherd to bring home those who were not yet in the fold.

The children?—Natalene lives in Scottsdale, where she's a light engineer. Tammy lives in Standing Rock but works in Window Rock, Arizona, as a contract analyst for the Navajo Nation's Department of Transportation. Geraldine is an artist in Taos—you can see some of her paintings online. Virginia works for the Navajo Nation in social services. Tommy, Jr., the only boy, works in electronics in Phoenix. Natasha, the baby, like her father, works as a gas engineer technician for Navajo Tribal Utility in Fort Defiance, Arizona.

And, yes, five Tso grandkids attended Rehoboth this year.

That tiny adobe chapel at Toyee has been gone for a year now, but things that happened there—like the time five Tso kids and their mom were baptized—have never been forgotten.

There's something fitting in the Tsos' return to the home place, to the shepherding both of them left behind years ago already. They're back home again, safe within the kingdom of the Lord.

And today they know the Good Shepherd—in head *and* heart—because he's the One who brought them home.

CHAPTER 7

Tribal Leader, Tribal Elder

Ed T. Begay

If you're interested in a leisurely lunch someplace in Gallup—say at Earl's or El Rancho—don't sit across the table from Ed T. Begay. Mr. Begay attracts friends and well-wishers, and even a few tribal lobbyists, like bears to honey. He knows most everyone, it seems, even though the Navajo tribe, the largest in North America, boasts nearly 300,000 people. No matter. Don't expect any peace if you're with Ed. People—hundreds of them, even thousands—know him and revere him.

That's because Ed has been their man in Window Rock for almost fifty years. Ask him a question about tribal politics, and he'll know not only the arguments but also the people advocating those arguments—many of whom he's known for decades. He started as a tribal council delegate from the Churchrock and Breadsprings chapters and served in that position for twenty years, during which time he rose to a number of leadership positions: he chaired the Advisory Committee, the Budget and Finance Committee, and the Education Committee, in addition to serving as a county commis-

Ed T. Begay

sioner with McKinley County and the New Mexico State Highway Commission.

That record of leadership brought him to some of the highest positions in tribal politics, as vice chairman of the Navajo Nation (1982-1987) and eventually as speaker of the Navajo Nation Council (1999 to 2003). Council watchers would likely suggest that

Ed Begay, tribal leader

the job of speaker of the Council is analogous to the team quarterback, arguably the most powerful position in local government, the speaker being most responsible for getting legislation to the floor.

The list of his political offices goes on, but simply listing titles doesn't explain the popularity and respect Ed T. Begay has earned through the decades. The word *politician* comes packaged, frequently, with substantial unsavory connotations, both on the reservation and off. Call someone a politician and most people picture a conniver: someone who talks a great show but rarely delivers, someone with suit pockets as expansive as the ones on cargo shorts—maybe even a thief.

And although a list of elected positions and offices held doesn't turn anyone into a statesman, what he (or she) does with those positions does. Just for a minute, let's take

a look at what forty years of public service translates into for Ed T. Begay:

- Government transparency: created amendments to the Ethics in Government Law to ensure that financial disclosure problems are resolved not politically but judicially, by the Supreme Court of the Navajo Nation.
- Government efficiency: merged various arms and branches of tribal government, creating a leaner, less expensive national politics.
- Tribal rights: sponsored legislation that charged Congress with more clearly defining the particular jurisdiction of the Indian nations.
- Maintenance of cultural values: sponsored legislation opposing new mining operations in areas reserved for sacred ceremonies; argued that the Council of the Navajo Nation has too often neglected its traditional code, the Navajo common law, and then initiated a study to determine the "Fundamental Law of the Diné."

In short, Ed Begay's record of service witnesses to the fact that through all those years in Window Rock, Washington, Santa Fe, and Phoenix, he was far more than a politician—he was a statesman.

The Story

But underneath all that, just who is Ed, the man who attracts a crowd almost wherever he goes? He was born in 1935 in the vicinity of Mariano Lake, some miles northeast of Rehoboth, on a broad stretch of grazing land owned by his grandfather. This was a significant chunk of New Mexico soil that ran right up to the place where the Red Rock ends, just across old Route 66 from Rehoboth Mission School. For as long as he can remember, he was a neighbor to the mission. Ed's mother died just five years after giving him life; not long after her death, his father left him in the care of his wife's parents, Mr. and Mrs. Tom Jesus.

This was one of the most respected families in the region. "In the twenties," Ed says, "my grandparents had a lot of sheep and goats: a thousand head of goats—that's a wealthy spread in those days—about nine hundred head of sheep." In addition, Mr. Jesus (pronounced *hay-soos*) owned about a hundred horses and two hundred head of cattle. On the Navajo reservation back then—not to mention in Iowa or South Dakota—those numbers were nothing to sneeze at.

Simple proximity to Rehoboth made the mission itself an ordinary feature of family life in those days. Ed's grandfather rented pasture land from the mission and often sold them meat for the kitchens. Relationships grew. Grandpa Jesus and Jacob Bosscher, the school superintendent—in effect the CEO of the entire operation from 1909 to 1954—became fast friends. They learned to bargain well with each other. "After all," Ed says, with a cagey smile, "my grandfather didn't give his meat away."

While Tom Jesus and his wife were committed to the old ways, they were also convinced that the education offered by the Rehoboth school for Navajo kids was a commodity not to be overlooked. Aunts and uncles—including Henry Jones and Irene Wilson—had attended Rehoboth school years before it became an option in Ed's own life.

In 1945, when he was just nine years old, Ed's beloved grandmother died, and he fell into deep sadness. Like his mother before her, his grandma was a woman he'd loved

Families highly valued their sheep.

dearly. The absence created by her passing brought him deep pain, he says, and fear—fear of dying and, as is traditional in Navajo culture, fear of death itself. When Ed told his grandfather he was afraid, he assured him that if they had a good year with the sheep, he would see to it that Ed would enroll at the mission school, a place with a whole different view of death and dying. It's a story Ed tells with tears in his eyes. Ed says his grandfather had come to understand the importance of the good, strong education his grandson could get at the mission, a place he had come to respect through a long record of honest business with good people.

"My grandpa said, 'You have to go to school,'" Ed remembers. "'You have to learn the white man's language. That way we can be in our world—the Navajo society—as well as in the white world—the *bilagáana* society." His uncle used to say that attending

Cecilia Damon

Rehoboth meant being able to integrate into the pervasive Anglo society, quoting the line "When in Rome, do as the Romans do."

Ed's uncle and aunt filled out the necessary applications. His grandfather hitched the horses to the wagon and drove him with one little suitcase to a place that wasn't all that unfamiliar.

Eleven years later, in 1956, Ed graduated from Rehoboth High School. Soon after, he continued his education at Calvin College, in the United States Army, and later at Albuquerque Business College. He married his high school sweetheart, Cecelia Damon, raised a fine family, and just recently retired from a long and illustrious career in tribal politics. Ed T. Begay has led a wonderful life.

Ed's wife, Cecilia, came from a family of particular significance herself. Her father, Nelson Damon, served as vice chair of the Navajo Nation in the late sixties and undoubtedly nurtured his son-in-law's ambitions for service in tribal politics. Cecelia was a highly respected nurse who held a variety of positions in the medical field. Her death in the late nineties was a profound loss for him, and her passing was mourned by many.

Attending Rehoboth was an important step in Ed's young life—of that there is no doubt. Yet he'll tell you in no uncertain terms that leaving his family to come to school, even though that family was just down the road, was an immense shock, as it was for all the Native kids. Suddenly he was out of his element—snatched from the sheep and the goats and the open range he'd known so intimately as a boy and swept into a completely different world.

The Long Walk

Navajo under guard

Tribal Heroes

Despite his parentless childhood, Ed T. Begay is a man with an immense heritage, which includes a notable Navajo leader—a man whose own mission in life, after a fashion, parallels his own.

Sometime in the early to mid-nineteenth century, a raiding party of Apaches in southern New Mexico grabbed a Mexican boy from his family and made him a slave—a common practice at the time. That boy was just thirteen when, not long after, the Apaches traded him to the Navajos for a fine black horse. The Navajos kept the boy and taught him their language. They gave him a name—Bi'éé' Lizhin, or "Black Shirt"—and even membership in a Navajo clan, Áshįįhí ("Salt"). With his newfound knowledge of the Navajo language, along with his native Spanish, Black Shirt was able to find work as an interpreter. According to custom, the boy's name was changed from Black Shirt to Interpreter, and, in the mid-nineteenth century, he performed valuable service for his adopted Navajo people in their volatile relationship with the whites, the *bilagáana*.

In Navajo history, Adiits'a'í is known as Jesus Arviso, the translator who worked diligently for the tribe in the darkest hour of their greatest horror: the times before, during, and after their incarceration at Fort Sumner, or Bosque Redondo. This was the time when the *bilagáana* determined that the best way to deal with the Navajo people was to put them all on a reservation across the territory from their ancestral homeland, and there teach them to be white.

Jesus Arviso was Ed T. Begay's great-great grandfather. Like almost all Navajos, Jesus Arviso suffered at Hwééldi, at Bosque Redondo. But all the while he worked tirelessly to advance the cause of the tribe, and, years later, bring the people home again. Every Navajo knows the experience of the people at Fort Sumner in the 1860s: the immense suffering and innumerable deaths that occurred on the death march to eastern

New Mexico, the starvation and despair that characterized their four-year stay on that naked plain, and the injustice the people suffered throughout. Most Navajo families today have a story that links them with "The Long Walk," but Ed's story links him with a central player in the Navajo's most significant tribal stories.

Once the people had joyfully returned to their ancestral homes between the four Sacred Mountains, Jesus Arviso collaborated with Dr. Washington Matthews to record authentic Navajo cultural ceremonies, practices, and legends. Both men understood that unless someone recorded the old ways, Navajo life itself would be in danger of disappearing in the tsunami of Anglo culture that threatened on every side.

The Boarding School Experience

Ed T. Begay's legacy of service was not just something he learned from his Christian education at Rehoboth. Servanthood was already in his DNA, in his blood, in his heart. As we've seen, his great-grandfather was an authentic Navajo hero, a historic figure in tribal history. His grandfather, a man of great wealth, mediated every kind of dispute that arose on the reservation—financial disagreements, failing marriages, and land rights. Ed remembers hearing his grandfather and some supplicant at the door talking in hushed tones, then moving to another, more private spot to consult.

That a man with such a significant Navajo cultural heritage might feel some resentment toward the disciplined regimen Rehoboth inflicted on young Native students during the middle decades of the twentieth century should come as no surprise. At best, Ed T.'s grandparents tolerated the Christian education Rehoboth offered. He remembers that

Daily regimens at Rehoboth were sometimes reminiscent of the military.

his grandparents believed in Navajo traditional practice "through and through."

But this deep adherence to Navajo religion didn't mean that his grandparents turned their back on occasional visits from the Reverend J. R. Kamps, one of the early Christian Reformed missionaries in the area. Ed remembers that Rev. Kamps "would come to our camp and there would be traditional ceremonies going on, and Grandpa and Grandma would set up a chair for him." In a short break between their own rituals, "they'd look at him and say, 'OK, do your thing.' And he did."

Some family member—maybe his uncle or aunt—would translate what Rev. Kamps had to say from English to Navajo, and occasionally Kamps would bring along a translator himself. "He'd sing and read the Bible and pray," Begay says, "and then, when he was done, they'd say respectfully, 'OK, you're excused.'" Entertaining the missionary was his grandparents' way of being friendly and polite, and maybe even learning something, says Ed. But they were not interested in giving up their own traditional Navajo religious practice.

Those were the attitudes and the belief system that Ed—just ten years old—carried to boarding school in 1945. "I didn't know a word of English—didn't get a word of what people were saying," he remembers during those first difficult days. Older Navajo boys would translate occasionally, which helped, but it was the military-like regimen that really bothered him—marching off to dinner, marching off to school, marching off to church, two by two, like cavalry. Even though all that marching and discipline made it easier for him to serve in the military a few years later, he says, it's clear that it was, and is, an irritant.

In those days, he remembers, the teachers made all the kids memorize the Heidelberg Catechism, as they themselves had done as children. Such unflinching commitment to what seemed to many of the students to be meaningless religious ceremony made some people, he says, simply "go through the process," and a lot of people resent that today. Explaining why some Rehoboth graduates feel dishonored by the education they received back then, Ed says the implication was often pointed and blunt: "If you don't do this, if you don't do that, you're going to hell." He remembers that one day, when some student asked a teacher to explain hell to them, "nobody could explain it fully."

The full effect of this Rehoboth education on Ed T. Begay is complex. It has produced memories that are as heavy-laden with shame and even anger as they are with the love of teachers and staff he and his wife will never forget. Throughout their years together, Ed and Cecelia drove miles from home in order to visit old teachers and friends from their mission school years—all the way up to Lynden, Washington, just to visit a woman who had lent them her car for dates now and then during their high school years.

Making peace with a cultural tradition that has decimated your own is not an easy task for anyone. Especially when you consider that, today especially, many Navajo people believe without question that Christianity is nothing more or less than the religion of the white people. So it's no surprise that for some people, acceptance of the Christian faith simply represents another chapter in the saga of cultural genocide Native people have already suffered.

RACHEL KASS

Ed Begay with grandchildren

Advocate for Tribal History and Traditions

People know Ed T. Begay, and they respect and love him. Take him out to dinner and see for yourself. Throughout his lifelong career of service to the Navajo Nation, he has been a representative of all the people, not only the Christians of the tribe. He has learned to weigh his words cleanly and thoughtfully in a way that honors all of the people and acknowledges their dignity, whatever their core beliefs and religious practice. He continues to be an advocate for tribal history and traditions.

Today Ed is happy that his grandkids are attending Rehoboth Christian School. Despite grievances, despite his criticism of the ways Rehoboth operated when he was a boy, he and Cecelia sent their own two children to Rehoboth when they were school age; and today, one of his daughters is sending her children. When the new Physical Education Center was opened recently, he watched his grandkids, in concert, carrying all the trophies from the old gym to the new one. He shook his head in wonder and gratitude. "To see it go on to the next generation," he told someone standing beside him, a tear in his eye.

Why did Ed send his own children to Rehoboth, having suffered the way he did at the mission school? "Because Rehoboth offers a very sound academic education, and we wanted to have our children educated so that they can go to any college or university in the United States," he'll tell you.

And they did. Ed's children have become successful in vocations that make a difference in the world. Sharlene Begay Platero went to the University of New Mexico and earned a degree in marketing. Today she works for the Navajo Nation in economic development. Her husband, John, works at the refinery east of Rehoboth. Sharlene served as chair of the Rehoboth Christian School Board for several years and was recently re-elected to another term.

Sandra Begay Campbell lives in Albuquerque. She's a structural engineer with an undergraduate degree from UNM and a master's degree from Stanford. Today she works at Sandia Labs and consults with many tribes on solar energy and wind energy. Sandra has served for six years on the Board of Regents of the University of New Mexico.

Sharlene and Sandra's record of service bear witness to the track record their father attained—both in tribal politics and in the church. In his local church, Gallup's Bethany Christian Reformed, Ed has served as elder on several occasions and held positions on denominational boards, particularly Christian Reformed Home Missions. Today, he is active in classical work and seeks to help Rehoboth get funding from the Navajo Nation. He is a faithful churchman.

Too often, he says, we don't care to live with other people—even good Christian people—from outside our own racial and ethnic communities, thereby breaking down walls that otherwise separate us as human beings. "We need to make the effort to blend in with a different culture, not to eradicate it," he says, "and on that job, there's still a lot of work to be done. Native people need to learn their own languages, their own culture, he explains, but then they also need to learn French, Spanish, and other languages so they can function in any of those societies as well." It's a lesson that runs deep in his own family's history.

But what about the heart of the Christian faith Ed was taught, the faith he was forced to memorize so long ago in school? A faith so often at odds with traditional religious practice on the reservation? What does he think of the words of Jesus Christ?

"Too often it's here"—Ed points to his lips—"but not here"—he points to his heart. That assessment comes out of a lifetime of political work, of attempting to balance the claims of widely differing cultures, of devoted churchgoing, of committed family life. "Loving Jesus and knowing Jesus—all of that has to take you somewhere," he says, "or else it's just not real." Trying to really live that way—living for Jesus—he says, takes a conscious effort.

You may hear a hundred people talk about "living for Jesus," but when Ed, a true leader of his people, talks about it the way he does, it's impossible not to see and know that what it really means and requires is not at all simple.

In 2002, Ed ran, unsuccessfully, for the position of tribal chair. One of the planks on which he ran was clearly from his own Navajo culture: "Elders must be respected as they possess knowledge and experience that are invaluable to the Navajo society. They possess the values and traditions of the Navajo people. They are the cornerstone of any strong family." That statement wouldn't be any less true if the word *Navajo* were dropped from each sentence. Ed T. Begay is, for all of us, one of those elders.

If you go out for lunch some time with Ed T. Begay, be prepared to be interrupted by many visitors. But when it's over, be sure to pick up the tab. It's a privilege to be at the table with him.

CHAPTER 8

The Holtsoi Heart

Flora Johnson, Mary Holtsoi, and Flo Barton

T his is a story of three strong women, three aggressive women, three purpose-driven women—along with a couple of very good men.

It's impossible, really, to separate any one of these three women's stories from that of the others. You simply can't know Flo Barton without knowing her mother, Mary Holtsoi, or Mary's mother, Flora Johnson, who died in 1996 at the age of ninety-six, as strong as ever. Although generations separate them, a certain force of character is something they all share.

To understand these three, you also need to understand the role that strong women have played—and still do—in the lives of Navajo people. Even today, it's often the women who hold things together, the women who take hold of responsibility itself, the women who largely determine the course of the family's welfare. Such matriarchy may well be a carryover from the days of nomadic living; in the clear distinction between male and female roles in that kind of life, the women had charge of the household.

Flora Johnson and Mary Holtsoi

Today, Mary and Flo laugh at themselves when "strong women" are mentioned. They look at each other and giggle knowingly, but they acknowledge that some people—men especially—might well consider all three of them to be *asdzání bóhólníihii*, "bossy women." Mary and Flo are more than

81

The Rio Puerco

a little proud of that description—never mind the negative connotations—because they know very well that without women taking control, a family's destiny can all too easily fall into ruin. When these women set their minds to something, the best policy is to play along or get out of the way.

Grandma Johnson

Flora Begay Johnson got an education at a time when most Navajo girls stayed home to tend the sheep and goats. Way back in the 1920s, she went off to Albuquerque Indian School, where she likely first heard about Jesus Christ and the religion associated with the white man. She went through nine grades at Albuquerque before returning to the reservation. Then she married Hiram Johnson, originally from Tuba City, Arizona, whom she'd met at school.

In the 1930s, Flora Johnson worked and worshiped for a time at a Seventh Day Ad-

ventist mission compound—a church, an elementary school, and a hospital—near Smith Lake. That's where her daughter Mary was born, and where Mary first went to school.

When that Adventist mission folded, Flora and her husband and daughter went off to Gallup, where there was work. Not for a moment was Flora Johnson afraid of work. She and her family found employment in the homes of European families who'd come to McKinley County for the coal in the mines just north of town along Gamerco Ridge. When Italians wanted only their own diet of tomato-y food, Flora learned how to cook Italian food—and she brought the recipes home. Her granddaughter, Flo, remembers eating pasta dishes none of her friends had ever heard of.

By day, Flora Johnson took charge of the cleaning crews that kept up some of the motels along Route 66, acting as housekeeping manager while pitching in herself with both hands. "My mother never finished her schooling," Mary says, "but she acted like she went to college." And then she laughs, as does her daughter Flo, because it's true: Flora Johnson rather liked taking over. She was a strong woman.

At home Flora also ran a tight ship. Everyone in her multigenerational family had tasks and responsibilities. Every Sunday, the whole troop would march off to Bethany Christian Reformed Church across the tracks and "the perky"—Rio Puerco—the swath of open land (which can quickly become a river) that separates north Gallup from the strip on Route 66 and the south. Flora Johnson made sure her family all went to church. She wrote the rules in the household.

Flora and Mary and Flo—grandma, mom, and daughter—started attending Bethany Church sometime after World War II. A small Adventist Church in Gallup had floundered and died, and one day Rev. D. E. Housman and Stewart Barton Sr. went door-to-door throughout town, leaving tracts and inviting people to worship. Soon enough, Flora gathered up her household—her husband, her daughter-in-law, her daughters, her son, and her granddaughter—and started marching off to Bethany, twice every Sabbath, starting a tradition of commitment and faith that continues among many of her descendants to this day.

Flora was even strong in the face of difficulty. After the Korean War her son, Jimmie, came to live with the extended family. What Jimmie had experienced in the military were things no one can see without suffering, and the years after his time in the Army/Air Force were not easy. Post-traumatic stress syndrome is a diagnosis that doctors wouldn't discover until years later, but that doesn't mean such a condition didn't exist after the Korean War. Back then, it was simply called "shell shock." Flora lived with her son's sometimes violent and dangerous behavior for years, always hoping and praying to bring him back to the man he had been before the war. Her prayers were answered. Today Jimmie and his wife are faithful servants of the Lord Jesus Christ who, almost every weekend on the reservation, attend revivals.

Mary Begay Holtsoi

When Flora's daughter Mary Holtsoi told her kids—all fourteen of them—to get an education, she wasn't kidding. She'd gone to school herself for little more than a couple of years. In her last year of school, one weekend she took a ride home from Crownpoint Boarding School to Gallup with a missionary preacher who was trying to get her and other kids to go to church there on Sunday. She rode along, went home to her mother, and simply never went back.

"I hated school—I didn't want to go to school," she remembers. "But today I'm sorry that I didn't." And that's why Mary Holtsoi, brimming with life at age eighty-three, told all her own children that they had to attend school. "You guys go to school," she told them, "so you're not dumb like me."

This self-assessment is obviously too harsh: Mary Holtsoi isn't dumb. She's blessed with the ample wisdom of age and all the life experience she's accumulated over the years, raising all those kids. What's more, she's as strong as her mother, strong and smart enough to laugh at herself, which makes her a joy to be around. Today she has thirty-eight grandkids and twenty-four great-grandkids. It's worth noting that nine of her children graduated from Rehoboth.

Billie and Mary Holtsoi and family

By the time she was in her twenties, Mary Holtsoi had already begun what would be a huge and loving family. Her first child was Flo, whose father, a Zuni, didn't know he was a dad when he left for the war, and didn't know he had a daughter until much later. Mary didn't tell him about baby Flo. Didn't think she should, really. Times were different then, much different.

But we're getting ahead of ourselves. There's more to tell about school, about some of the few moments when little Mary Holtsoi loved being there. Sometimes a Baptist preacher and his wife would come to the dormitory and talk with the girls about Jesus. Most of the kids had no idea what the two white missionaries were talking about, but Mary did. And when the woman asked whether anyone could recite the Bible, Mary Holtsoi proudly raised her hand; she'd been taught the Word in a tiny Seventh Day Adventist school at Smith Lake. She rattled off a whole string of Scriptures—from the Ten Commandments, she says, to Psalms 23 and 100, and even Matthew 5, all of it by heart. Because she could rattle off those verses as cleanly as she could, she got stars. Those moments she remembers fondly.

But the good times weren't enough to make her want to stay in school. When Mary Holtsoi left Crownpoint Boarding School for home, her mother quickly put her to work in the cleaning jobs and domestic positions she'd already staked out around Gallup.

During those years when Mary's daughter Flo was a child, Grandma Flora acted, in many ways, as her mom. This was not particularly unusual in Navajo households of the time. Grandma Flora filled in because during World War II, and for a few years thereafter, Mary was working as a Harvey Girl, a great job for a young woman at the time.

Back then, thousands, even millions, of young GIs were being shipped to California for deployment overseas. Along the way, they needed to be fed. Often those troop trains would stop at "Harvey Houses" throughout the Southwest—dozens of them. These were places that guaranteed good food and good prices. The Harvey Girls, as they were called, dressed in simple black dresses with a white collar, a black bow, and starched white apron—no jewelry or makeup. They acted, people say, more like hostesses than waitresses. In a way, the Harvey Girls were part of the war effort too.

Mary remembers how extravagantly those young soldiers tipped. She also remembers once spilling an entire tray full of dinners on some kid in uniform who, a minute later, turned the mess into a food fight that left everyone laughing. The Harvey Company frequently put its "girls" on the road to other Harvey Houses in Arizona or in Needles, California. Mary fondly remembers those years as being full of life and promise.

After the war, Mary met Billie Holtsoi at a "squaw dance," which was part religious ceremony, part social mixer. Her daughter

Mary Holtsoi with her grandchildren

Flo claims today that even as a child, Mary "had a good eye for men." Mary remembered Billie Holtsoi from fourth grade back at Crownpoint. And Billie Holtsoi would prove Flo's claim accurate—he was, in fact, a very good man, due in part to the influence of the women in his life and the Holy Spirit.

Soon Mary and Billie were married and the babies started coming along, one after another. For several years Billie worked on the railroad. He'd be gone all week long, returning on weekends to a house full of family that included a brother-in-law suffering through the pain of post-traumatic stress disorder, not to mention Grandma Flora. To Flora, her daughter's having chosen a mate from a squaw dance was unthinkable—as a Christian, she would have opposed all such gatherings. But remember: all these women are strong. Billie Holtsoi, not a churchgoer, crossed swords with his mother-in-law more than once. Many, many prayers were offered, Flo remembers.

Meanwhile, Mary Holtsoi was constantly with child—thirteen more after Flo arrived. Things started changing once Billie quit the railroad and found a job with the Bureau of Indian Affairs, and, later, the Navajo Nation. He was around more and was becoming a more integral part of the family. Neither Mary, his wife, nor Flo, his stepdaughter, knows exactly how or when it happened, but Billie Holtsoi began to realize that at least one reason his growing family wasn't falling apart was the joyful way the whole line of kids walked off to worship twice every Sunday. There had to be benefits there. Off they'd go—and Flo herself remembers what fun it was to head out with that growing line of kids, across "the perky" to Bethany Church.

At some point, by nothing less than God's grace, Billie Holtsoi started walking along too—first on occasional Sunday mornings, then more consistently, and then even on Sunday nights. Billie's drinking, which had been a problem, subsided and then just stopped. With great thanksgiving in his family, Billie Holtsoi became a believer and later a deacon.

God's grace moves mysteriously. Part of Mary's early attraction to Billie was his instinctive good nature, his sweet spirit, the depth of his heart. Billie was a quiet man whose warm smile and positive, accepting ways blessed the people around him at home, at church, and in the workplace. That character almost seems genetic, for to know the Holtsoi family is to see a common heart, one that flows from a dad and mom who lived out their faith with ample portions of joy and fun. "When we were little," Flo says, "we didn't have much, but we had lots of fun."

All kinds of work was going on in those days—no one ever stood still. Even so, there never was much money, not with fourteen kids and an extended family in a single small dwelling. Flo still remembers the immense surprise and elation when her stepfather brought home a ball—just an ordinary red playground kickball. She'll never forget how much they loved it, played with it until it required frequent patching. And one time he brought home the classic red wagon every kid of the era had out in the garage. Flo remembers how all the kids had to have rides—lots of rides, and how none of them could play with the wagon until they all were up and had finished all their chores. When you have so little, so little can easily become so much!

Mary Holtsoi and Flo Barton

This mingling of simplicity and provision marked the Holtsoi home. Son Darryl, now director of transportation at Rehoboth Christian School, speaks warmly of his dad's calling to provide for them. Billie's work for the Navajo Nation involved bringing utilities, especially water, to the community, and he took joy in being a provider not only for his family but for his people. Billie and Mary have shaped a family with a servant heart, and that sense of service has been passed on to the next generations.

Flo Barton

Once, when Flo Barton was working at the hospital, a nurse came to tell her that she really ought to go to visit a woman on her floor, a Zuni, who'd just had a baby. "She looks exactly like you," that nurse said.

And she was right. The two of them did look alike—in part because they shared a father. Flo Barton says that she resembles her father, not her mother; her mother says it's Flo's Zuni blood that makes her daughter

gab as much as she does. Whatever it is, the apple didn't fall far from the mother's tree either, because the two of them together have great fun. Their laughter and joy is contagious, as it must have been throughout their lives.

But like her mother and grandmother, Flo knows how to get things done. Today, whenever there are problems somewhere in the family, it's Flo who's called upon to arbitrate. It's Flo who gets called out of bed in the middle of the night. It's Flo who takes the bull by the horns when she can. Like her grandmother and her mother before her, Flo Barton is a strong woman.

Flo started her education at Rehoboth in the third grade and ended up graduating from high school, the first of the family to go to the Christian boarding school east of Gallup. That today she works as Rehoboth's alumni coordinator, that today she's as great a cheerleader as Rehoboth has, that she sings its praises, doesn't mean she hasn't known firsthand some of the difficulties connected with its past.

There are things she won't talk about, things she's suffered that she doesn't want others to know. Things that she's forgiven, she says, but never forgotten. Not once in all those years did she see physical abuse at Rehoboth, but she knew personally—even though she won't describe it in detail—mental and emotional abuse. It wasn't easy for a girl like Flo, just a child herself and part of a

Bethany CRC, Gallup

tight-knit, growing family, to be hauled away from those she loved and into the round-the-clock company of some she didn't.

The whole boarding school experience left deep scars in lots of Native kids, Flo says, and today she knows many Rehoboth alums who won't set foot anywhere near the campus. So much was required of them, she said, so much was force-fed—catechism and Reformed doctrine. And so much of what they had to do didn't have a thing to do with *their* will, what *they* wanted to do. In many ways, the boarding school experience didn't allow them to grow. It left bruises that have not disappeared, even though Flo has put them behind her.

Things changed in high school, Flo says, when school officials allowed students more freedom, and when clubs and organizations and sports teams created excitement and joy and community among the kids.

Still, there was tension. Two of her best friends—both white girls—made profession of faith when they were in high school; but

Flo simply wasn't ready. "That didn't mean I didn't love the Lord," she says. "That love was dormant—it hadn't come out yet."

At Bethany Church, Flo met Stu Barton, the son of the man who'd come door to door, inviting people to church, along with Rev. Don Houseman. Back in grade school, Stu was no friend of hers—he'd picked on her something awful, picked on her so badly that Grandma Johnson herself had to march over to the Bartons to tell them as much. Later, in high school, Stu dated all of Flo's friends, but not her. Sometimes, she says, she wondered why. Then he asked her out. And she said no. "That got his interest up," she remembers, smiling.

Flo and Stu Barton have been married for forty-four years now, and for just about all that time they've been happy. When they celebrated their fortieth anniversary, she told that huge family of theirs that at least thirty-five of those years were delightfully happy. That got a laugh, as well it should. It seems she and Stu Barton had some negotiating to do early on to determine who was boss. After all, Flo Barton comes from a long line of powerful women.

"I thought I should make all the decisions in the family, but in Stu's family it was his father, not his mother, who led," she says. So for a while "we fought like cats and dogs—it wasn't working." She shrugs her shoulders. "That's when we decided to start communicating and make our decisions together."

Sometimes even the strong have to let up a bit to survive, it seems, even to stay strong.

When Flo Barton started work at the Indian Health Service in Gallup forty years ago, neither she nor anyone else could have guessed that she'd be there for all those years. For a time she worked in records, and then in business, where the workload grew increasingly heavy. But even the strong have to throw in the towel sometimes. "God was working somewhere in there," she says. "I had to quit working because I could no longer keep up the pace. I must have been nuts to work so long."

Is Flo retired? Hardly. Today she spends a lot of her time at Rehoboth, her alma mater. And through all of it—through three wonderful kids, two of them very strong girls who take after their mother, their grandmother, and their great-grandmother—there was a man who complemented her and gave her balance. Like her mother, Mary, Flo had a good eye for men, and Stu was more than able to put her in her place from time to time.

Through all of it, Stu and Flo Barton, like their parents on both sides, have stayed with Bethany Church. "We've helped with everything," she says, "including playing the piano for worship, vacation Bible school, both serving on the church council, and lots of other things, and our love for the Lord became stronger and stronger and stronger." Finally, Flo and Stu Barton made public profession of faith and had their kids baptized—all in the same glorious Sunday worship service.

When Flo looks back on her life and her work and her mother—her mothers, in fact—and her stepdad, it all makes good sense. "When I was younger, I did not really understand what God was preparing for me. Never did I ever think that once I graduated from Rehoboth, I would return," Flo says. "In 'retirement,' I have been Director of Alumni Relations for two years—it was hard to decline an offer from Ron Polinder. The staff and students at Rehoboth have become my extended family. I have grown in my faith."

And then she reflects on the legacy of the two strong women who've deeply affected her life. "My grandmother and my mother were unwavering. Their faith in God was always so strong. I have a husband and a church family at Bethany who I must thank God for. I come from a huge family who have all been taught the Word, and have been taught to serve. God is good."

As everyone around them knows, there's just something about that Holtsoi heart.

CHAPTER 9

Citizens of the Kingdom

John T. and Emily J. Lee

I n many ways, John and Emily Lee's life stories are like bookends. They're well into their forty-sixth year together, despite the fact that theirs is what some might call a "mixed marriage"—John is Navajo and Emily is Zuni. The rich history of the Zunis is the story of a pueblo people, their history shaped by a community that's been planted in the same soil as long as any community in North America. Navajos, on the other hand, were semi-nomadic. There's a long history between the two peoples, much of it not peaceful. But both John and Emily come from good parents—fine, caring, moral folks, good members of their clans and tribes.

John's Story

When John Lee was five years old, his family lived in a small frame house his father had built, with a traditional hogan out back. John's mother, Sally, was a Christian; his father, Tom, was not. They and their ten children lived in the settlement of Beclabito, west of Shiprock, just south of Teec Nos Pas. Beclabito is a village that might well be

John and Emily Lee

described as a family compound—a circle of families in a few dwellings, just about everyone related by blood and clan. In the Navajo family way, John Lee grew up with myriad brothers, sisters, mothers, and fathers.

New Mexico's late-summer monsoon season sometimes turns the broad dome of

Zuni Mountain

desert sky into a snarling, flame-throwing beast. Storms rise up like fists to beat on the land. They depart just as quickly, creating whitewater torrents down arroyos that, minutes before, had been parched chutes of red dust.

One day just such a storm came up when John Lee was playing in the hogan behind his house. The world lit up as lightning struck the hogan, flattening John and two of his friends so powerfully they didn't begin to understand what had happened. Thankfully, no one was hurt, but the event stunned everyone. As was tradition, the medicine man was called.

There in the hogan, the medicine man began his work as custom and culture dictated. John remembers lying down in front of the people as the medicine man carefully created a sand painting in front of him in preparation for the ceremonies.

When he remembers that moment, he remembers too the way his father attempt-

ed, for a time, to keep himself positioned between two religious systems: his wife's newfound Christianity on one hand, and the richly familiar and traditional ways on the other. "Through the ministry of my cousins, the Redhouses," John says, "my father was being led toward Christianity, but he was caught between two worlds." It wasn't easy.

As the medicine man worked, John's mother returned from a Bible conference in Flagstaff, Arizona—a week of praise to God, of stirring messages and altar calls, a God-sent opportunity to renew the intensity of her faith. She walked into the hogan and there they were—her husband, her son, and the medicine man ministering to her boy, starting the series of religious blessings that could, traditionally, last as long as three days.

"Why are you doing this to my son?" she challenged, not quietly. She tugged at the Bible at her side, opened the pages to

92

something she'd marked, and pointed, as though the truth were there at her fingertips. "The Bible says God Almighty is the only true God."

John Lee remembers that moment well and says that his mother's determined objections altered something in his father's face and in his soul. "I don't know what else she said, but she influenced my dad right then and there," John remembers. Something changed.

Soberly, his father showed the medicine man to the door, then kindly brought him to his home. That experience was the beginning of a change in John's father. "The Lord just went to work on him right at that time," John says.

That change showed when a new kind of faith came to the close-knit community of Beclabito. A Lakota man introduced the Native American Church to the area—a movement that originated in the late nineteenth century and has spread through most of North America, with adherents numbering in the thousands. At the heart of the Native American Church is peyote, a mild hallucinogen thought to prompt spiritual visions. Its users say that most Christian believers talk *about* Jesus, but in the Native American Church—under the power of peyote—believers talk *to* Jesus.

The "Peyote Road" also calls for tolerance and togetherness between the Native nations, and its followers advocate for family care and the importance of gainful employment. The faith's tenets include mandates for living a highly moral life and refraining from alcohol and recreational drug use.

When the Native American Church came to Beclabito, John was just entering his teens. The introduction of a new system of faith, one that seemed far more Native than

white, held significant attraction for John, his siblings, and his aunts and uncles.

But not for John's parents. They opposed the use of peyote and were dismayed to see that some of the Native American Church's strongest adherents didn't hold to the faith's high moral standards. A neighbor, for instance, continued to beat his wife even though he practiced the new faith devoutly.

John's father built a home farther down the road, as if to deliberately avoid contact with what was becoming a force in the small community. However, when the distance between his family and the adherents of the new faith wasn't far enough—and an opportunity to move to a place closer to Shiprock arose—the Lees left Beclabito, their home, and their extended family. While this was a difficult time for the Lees, they found that their decision strengthened their faith, as difficulty often does.

Emily's Story

Emily's father, Andrew Chimoni, was a dedicated, traditional Zuni. He was a leader among his people and no small presence in the pueblo. He was an exceptional athlete, a champion marathon runner, a leader of his Kiva group, a songwriter. He knew the Zuni myths and the rich tribal histories. While Emily herself was a Christian, she says, "To this day, I don't condemn him for what he believed because so much of his teaching was and is still good."

When Emily's mother converted to faith in Jesus Christ, her father didn't want to leave his Zuni life, so the two of them made adjustments. "My father didn't like it at first, but the two of them loved each other despite their differences, and even respected each other's beliefs," says Emily.

Emily Chimoni

When Emily and John were married, her father told them that once they made a choice about how they would live, they should hold their truths earnestly and faithfully. "You stick with what you believe," he told them. "Growing up in my father's family," Emily says, "I learned the words *commitment* and *dedication*, and I learned them from him. I learned the importance of being faithful in what you choose—and having respect, too. Whether it was school or marriage or a job or being a parent, he taught us to respect leaders."

Today, Emily Chimoni Lee brings gifts to those family members who still participate in the ancient rituals of the Zunis, honoring her people, her friends, in that way, without participating herself. She's found a way to be Zuni *and* Christian. That generosity is something she may well have learned from her parents, who shared much of what they had with other Zuni relatives.

"Dad used to share all his produce with others," Emily remembers. "Our dad's strong values are instilled in my six siblings, too," she says. "The produce comes from the soil, and he truly believed that if you don't share, your crops won't be replenished." That was Zuni doctrine.

Attending Rehoboth High School wasn't a given for Zuni kids, but Emily had been urged to transfer to Rehoboth from Zuni High School by Winnabelle Gritter, a teacher at the Zuni Christian School, a woman who became a lifelong friend with whom Emily still corresponds. In fact, Miss Gritter took Emily home to Michigan for a summer so that Emily could work in a nursing home during the week and pick strawberries, beans, and tomatoes on weekends, all of which helped pay for her education.

Working on a Michigan farm took very little adjustment for Emily because her parents were farmers too—corn, squash, and

Zuni ceremony

The Lee family during their time in the Midwest

beans. She and her siblings had a wonderful childhood full of fun, but tending the crops was also a significant part of her early life. "We couldn't eat or drink until we hoed cornfields," she remembers. And she's thankful for that particular blessing of her childhood because a basic kind of morality existed then: "We had to contribute to endure," she says.

Their Stories Merge

One day in John's third year of high school at Rehoboth, everything changed—a new girl showed up at school. The guys in the dorm were all talking about her, but after they drew straws John was the one blessedly granted the privilege of walking the new girl back to the dorm. It worked. He

and Emily Chimoni, became, as they say, "a thing."

Her being Zuni and John's being Navajo didn't threaten their growing relationship in those high school years, largely because of the basic similarity of their families and their parents, who were determined and faithful. "We were both from hard-working parents," Emily says today. "We were both taught how to be a family and how to make a strong family. I saw that clearly in his parents, at their place—especially how to discipline your family, something shared from the value systems of both Zuni and Navajo peoples."

After graduation, John and Emily went to Albuquerque to further their educations. They continued to see each other and work together—and sing in the choir together—at Valley CRC where Scott Redhouse was pastor. That year, when an opening occurred in the Skeets Chapel, south of Gallup, John applied and got the job. They were married on October 3, 1962.

It was Pastor Ed Cook who urged John to get more education, to go to Michigan and attend Reformed Bible Institute (as it was known then). Emily had already lived for a summer in West Michigan; the idea of returning wasn't particularly traumatic. So they sold their car to raise money and hitched a ride across the country to Grand Rapids.

If you listen to them tell stories of that time, it's clear that those were good years. They attended Sherman Street CRC and liked it. Often they picnicked with Navajo and Zuni students studying in the area. It was a good life—John was at school, Emily took care of the kids (there were two girls by that time) and worked in a nursing home, earning a certificate for that work.

When John's program at Reformed Bible Institute ended, he enrolled at Calvin College in a pre-seminary program. He also worked at Keeler Brass, where he says he was surrounded by CRC people, not all of whom were as pious as the missionaries he'd known back on the reservation.

But he never quite made it to seminary never finished Calvin, in fact. A turning point came when he studied Native American literature one interim with a visiting professor from Texas. The reading assignments included a number of texts that advocated the kind of social justice other minority groups in America were working at, sometimes violently, during the 1960s. The book he remembers best is Vine Deloria's hugely popular *Custer Died for Your Sins: An Indian Manifesto*.

To say that reading the sad history of America's Native peoples changed John's life would not be inaccurate. For the first time, that history was opened to him in its stark and brutal reality—Custer, Sand Creek, Wounded Knee, the Long Walk. He wondered why such things hadn't been taught to him earlier, why he was so blind to his own history.

After surviving the holocaust, Elie Wiesel was angry with the God he knew from his childhood, angry about that God's absence from all the horror Wiesel himself had witnessed and suffered. John Lee, in his own quiet moments, asked the same questions Wiesel did: "Where were you in all of this, God? If you really love my people, where were you during all the injustice, in the violence, in the suffering?"

But while what he had learned about his history scarred him, John did not give up his faith.

With that new sense of their own story, John and Emily and their two daughters returned to Rehoboth. There was a job opening for dorm parents, and a deliberate attempt was being made to fill that opening

The Long Walk

THE MUSEUM OF NEW MEXICO

96

with Native people. For John and Emily, returning to Rehoboth meant having an opportunity to impart what they'd learned about Native American history to other Native kids so that they wouldn't be traumatized by stumbling on the truth the way John had.

What John had come to recognize in his studies of Native American life and culture was the irony and even the deceit of often well-meaning people who believed that Christians were the chosen people and that all Native people needed to become like them.

But what he never lost—or Emily either—was a commitment to Jesus Christ, whose love is always greater than whatever boundaries his people may impose in his name.

Home at Rehoboth

They've never left the faith, John and Emily Lee. They returned to Rehoboth in August of 1972, and they've been there ever since, ministering in a hundred different ways. Right now, John, 67, is working in the dining hall, keeping the place looking good. It's August, and it won't be long before all kinds of kids—Navajo and Zuni, Hispanic and Anglo, even a few exchange students—will be returning to the hallways.

Their two daughters, Marla and Darla, have given them enough grandchildren to keep them young. All of them attend Rehoboth. Two of them, Rainee and Andrew, live with John and Emily during the school year,

MARV SWARTZ

"Respect the mountains, the horses, the sheep"

an arrangement that might give some Anglo grandparents nightmares but isn't unheard of in Native communities. Emily says that it even comes in handy occasionally, when either grandparent is laid up with some malady or another. And besides, she says, it's the way the two of them like it. "I know it's a bit unorthodox for some of the families around here, but it's okay with us." A wry smile spreads over her face. "This campus became unorthodox when we moved here—that's my favorite line."

John tells one particular story from his past quite reverently. It's about his grandfather,

John and Emily Lee with grandchildren

Richard Red Goat, who one day asked his grandsons to come with him to the sweat lodge. "We just talked," he remembers. "It was after he became a Christian." The Native sweat lodge ceremony was the occasion for instruction and meditation. "He talked to us about everything—the mountains, the sheep. 'The mountain is yours; respect the mountain. Don't abuse the horses and the sheep, *She'ajaa',*'" he said, using a particularly intimate expression the boys knew was deeply felt and deeply meant. "He just talked about the whole creation— the water and the land. 'We won't be here long,' he told us, 'but the land will be here and the sheep will produce.' That's what he told us, and we sat there sweating, just sitting there together."

"Today," John says, "I say that to my grandkids too."

Many years ago, the mission program of the Christian Reformed Church was created under the title "The Heathen Mission Board." The word *heathen* comes heavy-laden with negative imagery, with decadence and debauchery. Staunch Calvinists, many of whom had been in North America for fewer than fifty years, perceived Native people as "the heathen" who were in need of conversion and assimilation.

But John and Emily, whose faith is real and evident in their lives, remind us that the word *conversion* has less to do with assimilation than it does with a reorientation of one's beliefs in the presence of a loving God.

The lives of John and Emily honor their own histories, their identity as Native people—Zuni and Navajo; but their God is the Creator of heaven and earth, of sea and land, and the Savior of those believers of every tribe and nation who come to him in faith. That faith is a gift they both cherish deeply.

CHAPTER 10

Open Door for One Hundred Years

The Bosschers

Kathy Bosscher wouldn't say it in exactly these words, but others might claim that her being the principal at Zuni Christian School these last few years was a divine appointment. After all, for most of the history of the Rehoboth mission, there have been Bosschers in western New Mexico. Kathy serves just an hour or so south of the place where her grandfather arrived, alone, one hundred years ago.

One of the things people like the Bosschers and Frylings and Vander Wagens lugged along to the new mission in New Mexico was a doctrine called "covenant theology." It's the belief, central to the Reformed faith, that God makes promises to his people, promises that include the children of the redeemed. No Calvinist truly claims salvation by DNA, but those early preachers and workers staked their lives on the belief that God would keep the promise to be their God and the God of their children.

It may be safe to say that Kathy Bosscher's "divine appointment" at Zuni proves that doctrine, but it's a story that still holds its share of wonder and grace. It's worth telling, in part because sixty long years separate the lives of Jacob and Nellie Bosscher and their granddaughter Kathy. Think of it this way—Grandpa and Grandma Bosscher grew up before World War I, in the early years of the century, while Kathy's own "years of discretion" came in the tumultuous 1960s, a world her grandparents had little chance to understand.

But here she is, and that's why some people might be more than happy to call her employment at Zuni Christian School a divine appointment.

Open Doors

Once upon a time, when Kathy Bosscher was no more than ten years old, her dad and mom—Art and Nip Bosscher—rounded up the kids, packed a lunch, and took them out for a day-long getaway, something they did quite regularly on Saturdays, she says. Her father's idea of a great time was to take off in some direction and explore. Somewhere in the course of an exciting day they'd get close to one of the many mission stations scattered across the reservation, and her parents would suggest they "stop in to say hello." She and her siblings would roll their eyes then, because they knew reservation hospitality virtually ensures that nobody just "stops in a minute."

She remembers dozens of such Saturday adventures, but one in particular stands out. That day they ended up at a mission parsonage. She remembers that particular day because she's come to understand that, in a way, it defines her and her family. That day, while Art and Nip chatted with the missionary couple and all the kids played on the porch, Geronimo Martin showed up—a man they all knew well, a Christian leader in the community. When they invited him into the parsonage for ice cream, Geronimo, the only Navajo, politely declined.

"Somehow I knew," Kathy says, "that he would not have said *no* if we'd been at our house." At the age of ten, Kathy saw something she hadn't seen before. Whatever reluctance the man felt taught her something about the way she and her siblings had been raised—there were no closed doors in the Bosscher home. We're talking genuine hospitality here—not simple courtesy or just plain being nice. We're talking gospel-enriched hospitality, an attribute born from a conviction that the image of God lives in every person who walks up to the door. "My mother believed in fairness," Kathy says unequivocally. The Bosscher home was always open.

Not surprisingly, Kathy's father, Art, and her Uncle Dave and Aunt Helen all remember identical behavior at their Rehoboth home an entire generation earlier. "We had guests at the table all the time—strangers would come, visitors, people from the whole community. They always came to

our house," says Helen. "Mother made oatmeal cookies by the hundreds, hundreds of cups of coffee." David, who spent fourteen years working for Christian Reformed Home Missions, ten of them as Field Secretary for Indian Ministries, remembers, "At dinner we'd be around the table—and here would come two more people. Immediately, we would go get two extra cups and saucers, and they'd sit down."

Art, Dave, and Helen Bosscher

Visitors from Michigan, merchants from Gallup, students and their parents, and just plain passersby—Jacob Bosscher and his wife, Nellie, had them all in. So did their own children, Art and Nip, a generation later. The whole family was blessed with the gift of gracious hospitality, doors always open, coffee always hot.

And after one hundred years in and around the Rehoboth mission, the Bosschers haven't changed—they're still loving and gracious, open-armed and open-hearted. They're still "people people."

Jacob and Nellie Bosscher

Because Jacob Bosscher, the Industrial Superintendent of the Rehoboth Mission, was in charge of every last business deal on the compound, salesmen would frequently walk into that wonderfully open house and greet a family that, by 1928, seemed to have at least eleventy-seven kids. "Mr. Bosscher," they'd ask, "exactly how many children do you and the missus have?"

He had a standard answer, according to his children. "Three and a half dozen," he'd say to his astonished visitors. Then he'd add, "Three girls and a half-dozen boys."

It wasn't always that way. Back in 1909, when Jacob Bosscher, a farm boy from Lucas, Michigan, arrived at the Gallup depot to take over the superintendent's job at Re-

hoboth, he was alone and unmarried. Just a year later, after little more than a post office courtship, he went on a pilgrimage back east to fetch Nellie Lucas, a Michigan girl, to be his bride. The "Just Married" sign was barely off the wagon when he took her west to a place she knew only by the descriptions in his letters.

Only a few degrees of separation stood between Gallup, New Mexico, and the "Wild West" back then. We can only imagine the worry in the hearts of those two young people's parents. On the Fourth of July in 1911, Jacob and Nellie Bosscher were moving a woman and her belongings out to a

Jacob and Nellie Bosscher and children

place called Two Grey Hills. It was monsoon season in western New Mexico, not a time to travel, but off they went. The rains came, the arroyos overflowed, and the rutted path became the Slough of Despond. The wagon got stuck axle-deep in slick red mud so heavy that the three of them could do nothing but call it quits and spend the night beneath the open sky. Sound romantic? It might have been, except for a dozen coyotes howling up a fuss and a score of Navajo folks stopping to stare, some of them more than a little shaky from a long weekend in Gallup.

"Personally," Jacob Bosscher writes in his memoir, "I soon fell asleep, mid the distant howling of the coyotes; but for my wife, this was not so easy since she was not so used to such a way of living." A significant understatement.

From the get-go, by her husband's description, the new Mrs. Bosscher's welcome to Rehoboth was nothing to write home about. At four in the morning, when they arrived at the Gallup depot, no one was there to greet the newlyweds or buggy them six miles up the road to the mission compound.

There's more to the story that can be whispered now, a century hence. You see, back in 1909, for a year anyway, Jacob Bosscher was the only eligible young Anglo male at the fledgling mission school—the only one amid a half-dozen equally eligible young women. That Jacob had to go all the way back home to fetch a wife didn't seem right to some of the women already stationed there. According to family history, even after Nellie Lucas Bosscher moved in, some of those women, who considered themselves spurned, didn't make her life any easier.

Despite this inauspicious debut, the newlywed couple not only made it through the year but stayed at Rehoboth for their entire working lives. There they raised a healthy, active family of nine children and labored tirelessly to keep Rehoboth afloat even through the woes of the Depression years.

Let me rephrase that—Jacob and Nellie Lucas stayed at Rehoboth for *most* of their working lives. Jacob officially resigned his post and left on April 1, 1912, with his wife and their first child, Beatrice, the first Anglo baby born at the Rehoboth hospital. In his own words, "I could not do justice to the work and the boys whom I was supposed to train along vocational lines," he says. That situation developed because he was "not able to convince the [Mission Board] that I needed relief through more help." When help did not come, Jacob kept his word.

Little more than a year later—in July 1913—the Board pleaded with him to return to the mission field. "After prayerful consideration and talking it over with our parents," Jacob put his family back on the train and headed back to New Mexico.

Their second child, Arthur, was born that year. Not long after his birth, little Art came down with a bad case of pneumonia and actually stopped breathing. Dr. Huizenga used mouth-to-mouth to resuscitate the baby, then told the Bosschers "not to look for his recovery. Humanly speaking, he was beyond help." "But not so with the Lord," Jacob writes. "We earnestly prayed for his recovery, and the Lord *gave* [emphasis his] our son back to us." Some decades later, Arthur would begin his own distinguished term of office at Rehoboth.

One of history's great gifts is the opportunity it offers for a kind of second sight. Knowing what others have gone through makes our own loads seem lighter. To read through Jacob Bosscher's memoirs of those early days is to encounter stories as difficult to imagine as they are amazing to hear, stories unlike those their granddaughter might tell today, a century later. Although baby Arthur miraculously recovered from pneumonia, Jacob and Nellie's suffering was not over. Here's more from Jacob's memoir:

> Those were hard days. Beatrice had come down with whooping cough sometime before and was by no means over it. Arthur was about a month old when he became sick. After [he] was on the way to recovery, Mom would have him on her side of the bed in a basket and I would have Beatrice on my side so that I could raise her when she coughed. We had the oil lamp burning low on the dresser. No electricity in those days. Mother heard the baby squirm and saw a mouse running over his face. I don't know how I did it, but I reached over and grabbed a great big field mouse off him and fiercely threw it to the floor. We were so worn out and weary those days; only the Lord saw us through and gave us strength.

There was much more: Jacob writes about the futility of trying to farm the desert soil; minus-thirty-degree winters; an entire dormitory going up in flames; innumerable trips to town for supplies and to the reservation to pick up runaways; a flu epidemic in 1918 in which the Natives "died like flies even as they traveled on horseback on the trail." Rehoboth itself was not spared. "All the boys and girls came down with it" except one boy and one girl. Four children died.

And always there was the pressure of more and more students wanting to enroll. For years, Rehoboth kept a waiting list; for years, Jacob and Nellie were saddened that there simply was no more room for more kids. An underlying theme in the memoir is Jacob's realization that the entire mission could—and should—be doing so much more for the Native people. That urgency, and the mission's incredible potential, drove Jacob's never-ending campaign to grow and improve every aspect of Rehoboth's outreach. Not unlike his granddaughter, Jacob was passionate about his calling, even though, consistent with his time, the full measure of his zeal most often lies hidden between the lines of his memoir.

Always, in such a dry desert area, there were problems with water. Without a steady supply of water, Jacob knew, a mission can't exist. In 1929 he determined that as much as $20,000 would be required to drill a well—ten dollars per foot of drilling. Back in Michigan, his immediate boss, Dr. Henry Beets, warned him that such a huge expenditure could be money out the window should a new well not be located—a loss that could, in fact, spell the end of the mission. "Now *we believe in prayer and supplication*," Beets wrote Bosscher, "and I have thought that two things would be very desirable: First, that you ascertain from those who best know just where would be *the most likely place* to find water. . . . But secondly, the thought occurred to me that it would be a fine thing if *special prayer meetings* were held by you people in Rehoboth, that the Lord might guide you in selecting the place [all emphases his]."

Jacob Bosscher's children all attest to the fact that their father had nothing but admiration and love for Dr. Henry Beets. But some-

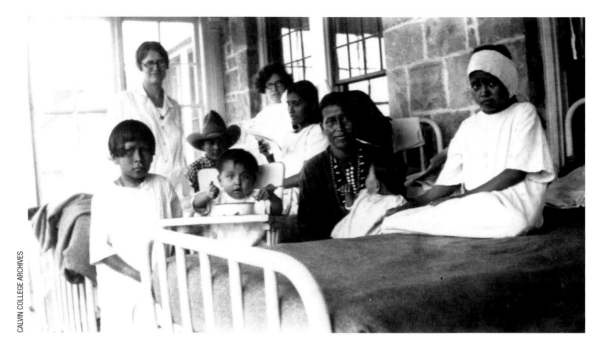

Patients at Rehoboth Hospital in the 1930s

thing in Beets's note tried Jacob's patience mightily. "Brother Beets," he responded, "I trust that we are not going to strike a dry hole." They'd been praying for water for six years already, he wrote, and he was confident he had done all he could. "I personally have no doubt but what we will get water, but it is about time that we are starting to work because prayer alone will not bring this well." He continued, "I hope the Lord's people will soon be made aware of the fact that the water is absolutely an essential thing, if this place is to continue."

There's feistiness here, a fierce dedication that won't be cornered. His granddaughter Kathy has it too, in spades. Clearly, Jacob Bosscher was a man called to his task, a man who loved the place and the people he and Nell served. That they were a dedicated couple who wanted only the best cannot be disputed. Jacob and Nell Bosscher's contribution to the mission is beyond calculation, not only because of the hard work they did

to keep the place afloat, but also because of the hospitality and goodwill they offered in the name of the God they so diligently served.

Art and Geneva (Nip) Bosscher

Arthur, the oldest son of Jacob and Nellie, graduated from "the Indian school," meaning Rehoboth, and went on to high school at Gallup. Back then, just getting into town every day required some planning. A man from Thoreau, east of Gallup, took a flat-bed truck into town every day, all winter long, and picked up kids along old Route 66, including Art, who piled into the back with the rest. Every day he'd march out to the highway where his dad had built a little coop to shelter him from bad weather. Healthy and wise, Art graduated from high school in 1932.

Art spent a year at Calvin College, in Grand Rapids, Michigan—a time he'd rather forget. "The folks couldn't really afford to send us there," he says. Besides, in West Michigan, he found himself in what he describes as "a strange culture." Art was a reservation kid with red New Mexico soil under his fingernails, an Anglo who'd grown up in the dusky shadows of desert mountains and pinion trees. "I hadn't been taught how to study," he says, remembering the high-octane scholarship required in college back then. "I was taking too many math classes—and I was homesick."

So he simply went home and spent the next six years of his life working for a Gallup wholesaler who sold supplies to the reservation—groceries, hardware, produce.

Then along came a young woman from Michigan named Geneva Knoll. Everyone knew her as Nip. Nip Knoll was accompanying a new missionary family as household help, and she caught Art Bosscher's eye so completely that he nearly refused to

let her out of his sight. Others hither and yon across the mission field noticed too. Dr. Pousma saw the spark between them and offered Nip a housekeeping job in the hospital, keeping her around Rehoboth once her first short tour had ended, and giving Art and Nip a bit more time together.

These two eligible singles spent a goodly amount of time together and snuck a few kisses beneath the clear New Mexico sky, but for whatever reason simply couldn't strike an accord. Nip left for Michigan in September 1938.

The whole story is delightfully told by their daughter, Kathy, in a memoir that retraces her heartstruck father's pursuit. Once a half a continent stretched between them, letters were sent. But even though a courtship by post had succeeded for Art's parents thirty years previously, nothing "forever" materialized between the young couple. So

Rehoboth Hospital in the 1930s

a year later, Art—who'd once found Michigan an "alien culture"—went back East with the sole purpose of fanning whatever flames still smoldered.

How things finally worked out was "most mysterious," says Kathy. Here's how she tells the story. Each morning during his visit to the Knoll house, Nip would go off to work, leaving her suitor behind with her mother "to chat the day away with her as he waited for Nip to return in the evenings. Wilhelmina [her mother] was charmed." Apparently her mother's being charmed warmed Nip's heart: "It startled Nip when she saw Art through the eyes of her mother. Then she loved him too." On February 19, 1942, Art finally married the young lady who had so totally swept him off his feet five years earlier.

Getting a job back east in the middle of the Depression wasn't easy, but Art signed on with International Harvester and eventually moved to Kalamazoo. Two years after they married, Art was called away to the Army, where he served from 1944 to 1946. By the time he left, Nip was pregnant with Rosemary, their first child.

Eventually, Art and Nip returned to New Mexico. Rehoboth—which is to say, his father, Jacob, the general superintendent—was putting in long-awaited central heating back then, new boilers for the residence halls. It was a mammoth job. "We were staying with my parents in their home," Art remembers, "and I applied for the job to run those new boilers." If two generations of Bosscher family historians can be trusted, it's fair to say that every last business decision related to Rehoboth requiring permission seemed to take forever. "Finally, Grand Rapids moved," Art says. "They said, 'You got the job.'"

Word eventually leaked out that "Grand Rapids" had been a little fearful of nepotism. "They were scared to hire me because they didn't want me working for my dad," Art says. They needn't have worried. "My dad would go out of his way *not* to help me," he says, smiling.

That was how Art started at Rehoboth and kept his hands in red New Mexico soil. He and Nip stayed there for thirty-eight years, the duration of their working lives. It's where the kids grew up, all five of them. It's where the kids went to school—a new high school at Rehoboth that Art himself had helped get underway.

And always there were those Saturday jaunts, family outings, ventures into unknown territory. By the time Kathy and her four siblings grew up, that same red New Mexico dirt was beneath their nails.

Kathy Bosscher

When Kathy left Rehoboth for Calvin College, it never crossed her mind that she might someday become the principal at Zuni Christian School. Returning to New Mexico was something she rarely thought of, even though her life "in the village" as she calls it, was almost idyllic. "Kids wandered the streets any time of day—it was a wonderful place to grow up," she says.

Kathy remembers wandering over to the playground during recess one day when she was no more than three years old and suddenly being surrounded by Indian girls who lived in the dorm. Her sister Rosemary, a year older, was with her, and her little brother Doug. All three were blue-eyed blondes, "three peas in a pod." The dorm girls went into a swoon. "Soooo cute," she remembers them saying.

When she left for college in 1964, Kathy's only goal was to get out and teach. Like her father before her, she worried about how much her education was costing. For that reason, she hurried things along to such an extent that she was able to graduate a semester before her friends. She'd always wanted to get into the classroom and make a living, longed for her own classroom with the kind of passion that characterizes almost everything she does.

But that's only half the truth. Here's the other half: Kathy wanted to be a teacher because she knew that teaching was a job she could do anywhere—emphasis on *anywhere*. Unlike her father, she felt no homesickness while halfway across the continent. If she fantasized at all, it was for distant shores.

Kathy wanted to see what the rest of the world was like, and she knew the first step to getting there was to put some money in her pocket. Her first job—a teaching position she picked up at the local public school—kept her right there in Grand Rapids, "deliberately." She started teaching in January, four months before her friends would graduate.

Kathy Bosscher did not fall far from the family tree, really. Her parents' and grandparents' unique gift and practice was to let anybody into the house—anybody, anytime. In a way, Kathy simply wanted to be the "anybody"—which is not to say she wanted to cash in on other people's generous hospitality. Instead she wanted to open the doors of her own heart for all kinds of people from all kinds of cultures.

In her words, Kathy wanted to "validate life," to seek out truly what life had to offer and make sure she wouldn't miss a thing. She wanted to validate her faith as well, to make it her own, not simply swallow it without question. She wanted to find out whether all this faith stuff was of real value in a far larger world than the one she'd experienced during her first twenty-one years. In retrospect, she says, her beliefs back then were sturdy, but she wasn't comfortable communicating those beliefs. Kathy Bosscher has always been the daughter of her parents and grandparents, but she's also a child of the sixties. She had to find her own way.

After a year and a half of classroom teaching, Kathy enrolled in grad school at the University of Michigan; she loved studying and wanted to get better at what she'd always wanted to do: teaching. Just two years later, she was teaching future teachers in a small, rural college in the Philippines as a Peace Corps volunteer.

Compelled by the rigors of Peace Corp training, which required its volunteers to live at the same economic standard as those they were tasked to serve, Kathy began to sort through her own childhood at Rehoboth. Visiting an old college friend who'd become a missionary to the people of the Philippines, Kathy says she was "appalled" at how affluent her old friend seemed in her cultural context. That wasn't the Peace Corps way. She became critical of what she calls "compound missionaries," those who live apart from the people they serve.

Wycliffe Bible Translators

When the locals began to point her toward some "Americanos" down the road, she avoided them like the plague; after all, she was in the Philippines for Filipinos, not to buddy up with more Americanos. But back in New Mexico, her mother, who was worried about her globetrotting daughter, engineered a meeting between Kathy and some friends of friends who just happened to live down the road on what was a Wycliffe compound.

Thus began a relationship Kathy has maintained with Wycliffe Bible Translators for decades. With Wycliffe, the Rehoboth missionary kid found a way to carry out mission work that harmonized with her own developing character. In a way, you might say, it was love at first sight. "Aha," she says, remembering. "Here's a group of people I could relate to because they were living in the community, doing a service, building relationships with the people—and they weren't in this . . . compound." She adds, "And it was great fun."

The Peace Corps teaching assignment left volunteers with a summer off, during which time they were expected to find a way to immerse themselves in the culture and build relationships. When Kathy proposed that she spend the summer with the Wycliffe people, the Peace Corps director was pleased, and she was in.

That first summer, what she experienced with Wycliffe was pure joy. Wycliffe workers were dropped into all kinds of exciting new worlds from jungle air strips. "You fly in," she says, "but then you're just dumped into the middle of things—wherever you're put down, that's where you live, that's where you are. I spent six weeks with the Wycliffe people that summer, and I had a blast."

Speaking of that first summer with Wycliffe, Kathy's joy and passion fill the room. Her eyes flash, her smile beckons, and her hands—and arms—slash the air as if she were some baton-wielding, over-the-top maestro. She can barely contain her enthusiasm.

That first summer's relationship with Wycliffe was a kind of courtship. The woman fell, head over heels, in love with a program that brought her directly into the lives of indigenous people who hadn't yet heard the good news of the gospel in their own language. The Wycliffe folks were not "compound missionaries" distributing mission barrel clothes; instead, they walked the same streets, ate the same food, and breathed the same jungle air as the people they served. They stayed in any shelter they could find.

Kathy was just twenty-six years old when her term with the Peace Corps came to an end, but by then she'd seen enough of Wycliffe to believe that her own education could help their outreach. "I think I was a typical smart-aleck kid," she says, chuckling, "but they seemed to think I was right."

The Wycliffe program includes teaching, of course, and there Kathy found a place. Her job was structuring a program to teach local people—most of whom were barely literate—how to teach their friends and neighbors how to read. It was a broad literacy program aimed at opening up the Word of the Lord. For a recent grad of a respected program at the University of Michigan, a woman who'd already been teaching future teachers in the Philippines, the job was a perfect fit.

The Wycliffe model for missions was wonderful, Kathy says. "It reconciled me to a way of doing missions that was authentic and did not smack of paternalism, or capitalism, or colonialism—all the nasty ideologies she felt had too often affected the outreach of western Christian missionaries.

Working with Wycliffe meant Kathy would have to raise her own support by signing up sponsors and churches willing to take collections. Rather than "be dependent on anybody," Kathy essentially sponsored herself by returning to New Mexico and getting a teaching job so she could make some money. "I knew I could live anywhere on the Navajo Rez," she says. "I could get a job there; I could live there; I could feel at home."

Thus began a pattern that extended through many years in the life of Kathy Bosscher—two or three years of teaching on the Navajo Reservation, then two or three years with Wycliffe at some far-off spot across the globe, then two or three years back in New Mexico. Multiply that four times, over a couple of decades.

The first Wycliffe stint was a field project: to develop a full arsenal of teaching strategies and materials for a people called the Kalinga in the Philippines. For two years, she stayed right there with the Kalinga. She set up the program and ran it as a model.

When she returned, Kathy taught for two years at Tohatchi, then returned to Wycliffe as a literacy coordinator. Two years in Asia, then back to the rez; two years in West Africa, then back to the rez. She'd barely pull her clothes from the suitcase before she'd be back on the road. She loved teaching kids on the rez, the place she's always considered her home; she loved being dropped into new and exciting places. She's had the best not only of both worlds, but of many worlds. In a word that comes up dozens and dozens of times as she recounts all this adventure, Kathy always had fun—not fun as in life on a playground, but fun as an athlete—hard, challenging, exhilarating fun.

Zuni

When Zuni's principal, Brian Kruis, heard Kathy was returning to the area to do some more teaching, he asked her to join the staff. Now Kathy Bosscher was born and

Zuni mission, early years

reared in McKinley County, New Mexico, a third-generation resident. For most of her life she's known the people who've staffed the Zuni mission. She's known Zuni students, both as a student herself and as a teacher. But she told herself that a job at Zuni—even temporary—wasn't for her because she didn't think of herself as "a Zuni person"—to her, home was the Navajo Rez. Zuni is different. Zuni is not on the Navajo Rez. What's more, Zuni Christian Mission School is *Christian*; her previous temporary teaching posts were in public or Bureau of Indian Affair schools. In a sense, she'd be coming home, but not really. And that created some discomfort.

To much of the Anglo world, Native life is all but invisible. Indians have casinos, of course, where they make big money, and they get to hunt whales and net walleyes when and where no white guy can. But distinguishing between tribes and nations is not something most white folks think about. Navajo? Zuni? They live, what—an hour apart? They've got dark eyes and hair and lots of jewelry. They're all Indians, right?

But those who live in the neighborhood know very well that Navajos and Zunis have separate languages and stories. Their two cultures share very little, and their tribal histories are completely different narratives—except where the two tribes have intersected. What's more, those intersections were not peace vigils, and therefore are not easily forgotten.

The characteristics of a people—be they Zuni, Navajo, Dutch, Irish, or American—can very easily slip into caricature. Human beings love to paint boldly, a single shade for an entire people. For all of us, prejudice colors our perceptions. But some characteristic behaviors actually help us understand

people, whether they're Dutch Reformed or Shiite Muslim.

The Zuni are pueblo people, small-town folks who've lived, by choice, in a tightly-packed adobe community for generations. Navajo towns are almost nonexistent. Historically, at least, Navajo people have tended to identify themselves geographically by landmarks, mountains or mesas, and more recently by chapter houses and trading posts. But Navajos need space for their sheep; historically, they were semi-nomadic. They were and still are deeply rooted in a region of the country most of them can pinpoint vividly, but within that expanse there's all kinds of elbow room.

Religion plays a significant role in the lives of both the Navajo and the Zuni, as it has in most human beings throughout all of human history. But anthropologists have long noted a difference. Zuni religion seems primarily preventative. The calendar of the pueblo is packed with religious ceremonies because the people believe that heartfelt piety wards off calamity. Prayer fends off evil spirits that will otherwise destroy people's lives. The power of Navajo religion, on the other hand, lies primarily in healing. When those disasters strike, the medicine man is beckoned to perform what he can to dispel the evil that already has found a place to abide.

Those kinds of cultural differences can create some discernable differences in behavior. To Kathy Bosscher, the invitation to come and teach at Zuni seemed a stretch, not because she didn't like Zuni people but because she knew and felt at home, as well as any third-generation white woman could, with the Navajo people, who abide in the very place she calls home. And back then, a teaching stint back home was something of a means to an end, a way of making enough money to volunteer once again for Wycliffe.

With all that arguing *against* saying yes, what changed Kathy's mind? In true, determined Kathy Bosscher fashion, *she* changed her mind. "I gave myself a lecture. What if God is calling you there?" she asked herself. And so the globetrotter trotted south to Zuni to check things out. "I realized it was going to be more work for me—almost like being dropped into a new culture in Africa or Asia," she says. "Moving back to the Navajo Rez wasn't any work—I mean, there are new people, but there's no need to figure out how to deal with people because you know them."

Two images made the case. First, when she drove into the Zuni Ministry Center parking lot, she was greeted by a two-year-old, the pastor's daughter, who seemed to have been left quite clearly alone. Immediately, it seemed to her that she was in the bosom of nothing less than a loving village. "Maybe we can do this," she remembers thinking at that moment.

Then there were the bacon, lettuce, and tomato sandwiches her hosts served, she says with that wonderful smile again—and she'd just come back from Africa. "I was impressed." And that's understatement.

Kathy Bosscher is not afraid of hard work. She inherited her drive from generations of missionaries and farmers and who knows what else, each of them pushed along by a Calvinist work ethic. At the same time, her primary motivation for living can be assessed very easily—she's always wanted

The Frylings, pictured here, and the Vander Wagens were the first missionaries sent to the Southwest.

CALVIN COLLEGE ARCHIVES

111

her life to be fun. Seriously. She's always wanted to love life. That she does goes without saying.

She took the job.

But the pattern of Kathy's life didn't change. She stayed at Zuni Christian for three years, then returned once again to Wycliffe and South Asia—India and Nepal, with occasional junkets into Africa—for another three. "I love India," she says, rolling her eyes, "that's my all-time favorite place."

In 1996, Kathy came back to the red soil and heard from those who loved her that not only was she getting old-*er*, she'd also, someday, come to regret never attaining any kind of pension. In addition, her mom and dad had come to that point in life when they could use an adult son or daughter around for occasional help. Once again, she was offered a job at Zuni. Once again, she decided to stay.

But there was no administrator at Zuni. Gord Kamps, son of the early pastor and a retired school administrator, stayed as a temp for a couple of years, when good administrators were hard to come by. But when, after a few temporary stints, Kamps declined an invitation to come once again, he talked Kathy into a one-year appointment, which she accepted—and that made four years at Zuni, longer than she had stayed anywhere for the last few decades.

Kathy had to make a decision—was she going to fully commit to Zuni and end that wonderful itinerant life? Zuni needed more stability than she could have given them, had she decided to continue her "here today/gone tomorrow" way of life, she says. She decided to commit. That was in 1999, and she's been at the reins ever since. "And I haven't been out of the country in . . ." she says, "well, it's been a long, long time."

Grandpa and Grandma—Mom and Dad—and Kathy

When she was a toddler, Kathy remembers the days when her mom would tie spoons to her children's wrists when they went out to play—after all, Nip Bosscher didn't want to lose those spoons. One day when they were there playing in the front yard sand— this is a family story, often told and retold— it was Kathy who addressed an elegant lady who walked up to the front door. This was a door they never used, which meant she had to be a stranger. When no one answered the doorbell, the elegant woman asked the girls, "Is your mom at home?"

Famously, Kathy told the woman, "Just go in. My mom lets anybody in."

Something of that openness, gregariousness, hospitality, even love, runs through three generations of the Bosscher story— love of people, love of red dirt beneath the fingernails, love of God and God's love for us. Something of that is there in the tales told by those who remember.

Watch Kathy in class with first-and-second graders lined up before her. Her arms are whirling, her face radiant. "Let's take a trip today," she tells the kids, as though they were bound for Nepal. She's picked out Carlsbad Caverns, across the state—but no matter. The kids tune in brilliantly, their eyes turn, on cue, as she tells them about hoards of bats in the caves, and about all that beauty.

The voice you hear in Kathy's class, like the voice you hear in her grandfather's memoir of the early days in Rehoboth, prompts that line from the book of Matthew about "the least of these my brothers and sisters."

Really, their lives couldn't be more different. Grandpa and Grandma Bosscher settled at Rehoboth at a time when the place

Kathy Bosscher teaching at Zuni Christian School

was as close to the Wild West as any you could find in America. Today Rehoboth—and Zuni—are only an airport from India, or Ghana, or the Philippines. Grandpa and Grandma would find it hard to believe.

And there's this.

"The thing that has kept me motivated throughout my life is a challenge in front of me," she says, "and here, at Zuni, I have not run out of challenges."

What kind of challenge specifically? "How can this little mission—how can I—be salt and light? That will always be the challenge. One of the things that I've found so intriguing and good is that here you must articulate faith in a way that is not just words. It must be real and dynamic and authentic. That, for me, has been a huge exercise in faith."

That's Kathy Bosscher, through and through. But I'm pretty sure Grandpa and Grandma, like Mom and Dad, would agree. Some things don't change.

CHAPTER 11

Women of Conviction

Clara Lauber and Karen Lauber Schell

W hen Karen Schell was just a girl, she would have loved to go to school at Rehoboth, she says, but it never happened. Why not? Well, for several reasons.

The Lauber family lived quite a distance down the road. Today, from the Chee Indian Store, the family business where Karen and her family live, it's almost exactly forty miles to Rehoboth school. But back then—when there was no I-40 freeway—forty miles took a long time to travel.

Another reason was money—or the lack of it. The Lauber children grew up beside a mission church as part of that church's vital life. Basically, Karen says, they wore what she calls "mission-barrel clothes" through most of her childhood. Harrison and Clara Lauber, her parents, lived frugally, not only because they had a meager income but also because their deep and abiding faith heightened their characteristic Navajo propensity for giving one's possessions away. In short, the cost of tuition was prohibitive.

But there was more, too. Karen, her sister, and her brother could attend near-

Karen Lauber Schell and Clara Lauber in front of the Chee Indian Store

by Sanders public schools and not leave the intimacy of a very tight, very devoted Christian family. Rehoboth would have meant boarding, and the whole boarding school idea, some argued, had weakened Navajo families by removing kids from the intimacy of their parents, while keep-

115

ing parents themselves from learning to be moms and dads.

Some old and precious family stories painfully recounted the horrors of boarding school operations. Karen's mother, Clara, remembers how her grandfather, himself a medicine man, told of the pain he felt when his youngest daughter, the baby of the family, was literally carried off to a boarding school in Ft. Defiance. Her grandfather's insufferable grief, or so the story went, got him up on his horse to take on a full day's ride to Ft. Defiance.

What Clara remembers best about the telling of that story is the searing memory of her grandfather's deep distress when he stood outside the fence of the boarding school compound, horrified by the image of a hundred indistinguishable little Navajo girls with short-cropped hair and Anglo

Dr. Richard H. Pousma

dresses. Today, Clara Lauber doesn't remember whether her grandfather actually spoke to his precious daughter that day or not. What she remembers from the story is her grandfather's agony. His precious daughter seemed lost. Such stories, told over and over and over, have abiding resonance.

In other words, there were good reasons why Karen Schell, along with her sister and her brother, attended Sanders public schools, even though they might have liked to go to Rehoboth. But then, there are also good reasons to explain why things have changed—why, since that time, Karen and her husband, Paul, have invested a great deal in Rehoboth. Their own children either have gone there or are attending now, and Paul and Karen put in tons of hours as school board members. Karen is just finishing six years on the Rehoboth school board, the last four as chair. "Other than my family and my work, Rehoboth has been my life," she'll tell you.

And it has. She and her sister Carol were born at the Rehoboth hospital into the capable of hands of Dr. Louis Bos, a man her mother remembers very fondly. For years, both Karen and her mom met Rehoboth people at the annual Southwest Bible and Missionary Conference in Flagstaff, where, often as not, CRC ministers and missionaries would be well represented on the speakers' rostrum.

Maybe even more important, Karen and her mother both maintain that Rehoboth and its alumni have created and maintained a record of distinguished service within the Navajo Nation. Some of the finest leaders of the Navajo people received part or all of their education at Rehoboth. "Rehoboth has always had a high reputation around here,"

Nana Lauber (center) with Harrison (far left) and others

Karen says, "because its graduates have been leaders in the reservation communities."

If the truth be known, the relationship between Karen Schell and Rehoboth schools predates even her own life. When her mother, Clara, was just a girl, she remembers her father, Denet Chee, talking emotionally about Rehoboth. Sometime early in the century, when he was just 15 years old and down with a virus he simply couldn't shake, he went to the Rehoboth hospital and was nurtured back to health by Dr. Richard H. Pousma, a man she says all the Navajo used to call *Hastiin azeetsoh,* which is to say, "medicine person who is large" (both in the sense of *important* and *not small).* "Years ago my father always used to tell me," Clara says, "that the medicine at Rehoboth always heals you, but the public health service doesn't."

Even though Karen never attended a day of school at Rehoboth herself, there are ample reasons to understand why she and her mother have become so loyal a part of the school and community.

How loyal? Listen to this: When Karen's daughter, Jennifer, has volleyball practice at Rehoboth, Karen regularly drives the forty miles into town to pick her up. Sometimes, for whatever reason, she has to wait. "I'm not the kind to spend my time shopping at Wal-Mart," she says, so she arms herself with a bottle of Windex, because, as everyone knows, the battle to keep school windows fingerprint-free is never-ending. "Janitors already have a lot to do," she says, so the board president spends a half hour or more with Windex and a rag.

But those who know Karen Schell would be quick to point out that Karen is a mover and a shaker. She gets things done. She admits that she likes telling people what to do. She started college in the nursing program at Biola University but found that she wasn't thrilled with "bedpans and all of that." So, a

117

few years later she transferred to Northern Arizona University, where she switched her major to something she found much more to her liking: health care administration.

So where did this full dose of heady self-determination have its origins? Karen says she watched her father, Harrison Lauber, mellow as he aged, become a different kind of father than he'd been when she was a girl—a loving, even doting grandfather. Even though he had been, for as long as she could remember, an active Christian (often busy around the mission), he had often been absent from his children's lives. But Harrison Lauber was always hard-working, sometimes maybe to a fault. He was no laggard, and he passed that industry on to his daughter.

Clara Lauber, Karen's mother, takes hold of life's problems. Active in her local tribal chapter, she attends its meetings regularly. When she thinks it's got to be done, she visits Window Rock, the tribal headquarters, to make sure the political leaders understand what's going on. She's as direct and strong as her daughter—or perhaps one should say her daughter is as direct and strong as she. Make no mistake: Karen and Clara are devoted Christians and have been for years and years. Even before she was old enough to drive, Karen took the church van up and down the dirt roads of the neighborhood, picking up parents and kids, grandpas and grandmas, and driving them to the Good News Church where Karen and Clara worshiped. Karen and her mother are

Good News Church

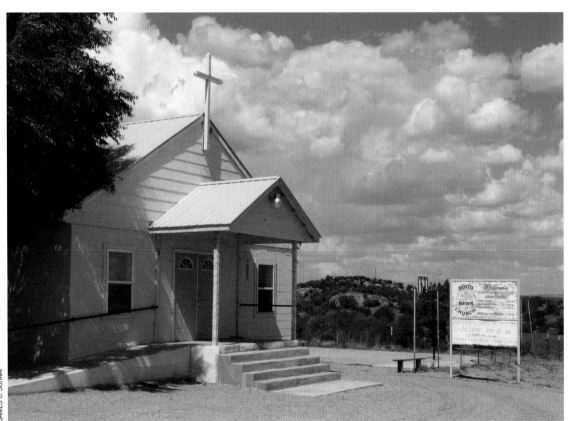

passionate about their faith, and not a bit sheepish.

Sheep may be a convenient metaphor here; after all, the Laubers have always had sheep and still do. In fact, for the most part, the flock that's left belongs to Clara, who still enjoys tending them and does her own butchering. If you walk behind the store, you'll still find a dozen or two sheep in pens. But neither mom nor daughter resembles, in any way, the sheep they tend—not at all. They're not passive or easily led astray, and they're fully capable of taking on the coyotes. They're diligent, hard-working Christian women.

And yet, if you want to understand them—to know them—if you want to hear their story, they'll resolutely begin its first chapter with a woman whose life was incredibly remarkable, a white woman who came to the reservation and never left—Clara's mother-in-law, Iva H. Lauber.

Just about everything one could know about Iva Lauber is written on lined papers and kept in scrapbooks tended by Clara and Karen. "She always wanted me to tell her story," Karen says, and she hasn't put the assignment aside. Before she died, Iva gave them all her notes and remembrances. And when Karen holds all those memories in her hands, the resolution shows in her face.

Nana Lauber

Clara and Karen have funded a Rehoboth scholarship in Iva's name and that of Clara's husband, Harrison—Iva's only child, an adopted son. Each year, sometime in November, Rehoboth students apply for that scholarship, and when they do, they read at least a bit about this woman. "Iva Lauber was a missionary on the Navajo reservation in Houck, Arizona until the end of her life,"

Nana Lauber with grandchildren Caleb and Karen

the scholarship announcement says. But the story behind that sentence is rich and big.

"Everyone called her 'Nana,'" Karen says of the woman who was her grandmother. In fact, she was "Nana" to so many Navajo that once upon a time a friend complained to Karen that she simply couldn't find Nana Lauber's name in the phone book.

Nana Lauber was Swedish, from Minnesota. But once she'd chosen the Houck region of far northeast Arizona she simply never left. Her story, embedded within the story of Karen Schell and her mother, Clara, should be better known.

Iva H. Lauber graduated with a degree in chemistry from a school in Minnesota, then went west to Biola College in Southern California, an institution whose name is an acronym that suggests why she attended: Bible Institute of Los Angeles. Like so many others in the early years of the century, Iva was listening to the call of mission work.

Once she'd spent some time at Biola, she and her husband went east to Ganado,

Arizona, and the Presbyterian mission there. Tragically, while serving as house parents, she and her husband lost three children, including twins, at birth. Not long after, Iva's husband became terminally ill, and they returned to California, where he too died. Iva Lauber knew what it meant to feel darkness at the center of her heart.

After all that loss and some time back at Biola, she determined that she would return to the Navajo reservation, alone and unmarried. Someone in California gave her a homemade house trailer. Someone else told her of a place near Houck, Arizona, that needed a Protestant missionary. So, determinedly, she set off east to the Arizona/New Mexico border, where like some explorer who has finally come to his anticipated final destination, she simply set down that makeshift trailer and began a ministry

that didn't end until August of 1986, when she died at 93 years old. Her life was her mission.

Even when she was old and crippled with arthritis, she still insisted on teaching Sunday school to the littlest Navajo children. She seemed to lack the skill for learning the Navajo language, but that didn't stop her. Both Clara and Karen remember her sitting around a table full of Navajo kids, all smiles, understanding nary a word that was being spoken. The Navajos called her *asdzą́ą́ bahózhóní*, or "happy woman" for her unceasing smile.

Eventually, she and others put up a church along old Highway 66, a place that's still there, just off I-40. That church—and the significant house beside it—became a refuge for kids from the neighborhood who were taking the bus to school at Sanders.

Nana Lauber teaching Sunday school

One of those children, Harrison, was less than ten when he told her that he would really like it if Nana Lauber would adopt him. Adoption was something she'd not done before, nor would she do again, but this little boy, she must have thought, was not only willing but needy, so she went through with it. That little boy grew up to marry Clara Chee and become the father of Karen Schell.

For years, Harrison and Clara—and their children—lived in a small house that stood right beside Nana Lauber's home, just beside the frame church that looks just like any other 40s-era reservation mission center. For years the Laubers drove the dusty reservation roads every Sunday and every Wednesday, picking up children and families, old and young, for worship services. For years the family sat through long devotional exercises at every meal. For years they heard about the evils of dancing, of card-playing, of going to movies. Karen Lauber Schell grew up in a devoted, pious family.

It was a wonderful, never-to-be-forgotten childhood, orchestrated by a white woman who brought heart, soul, mind, and strength into bringing the gospel to the Navajo people. The entire family worshiped and prayed, sang and spoke of the Good News. And when Karen, the eldest, graduated somewhere near the top of her class at Sanders High School, where she was awarded the annual citizenship award, it was Nana Lauber who urged her to consider her own beloved Biola.

But Karen's first year there was a near disaster, academically at least. She soon came to understand that the education she'd received at Sanders had left her woefully unprepared for college work, especially when contrasted with the American suburban kids who'd been through more rigorous academic programs. What's more, it was the 1970s, and the times, even within evangelical America, were a'changing.

She'd never heard of the Christian rock bands that regularly gave concerts most of her Biola friends attended and loved. In her family, rock music was "of the devil," but at Biola she heard Scripture itself fashioned with a rock beat. The first time she went to a movie—*The Jungle Book*, Disney's cartoon version of Rudyard Kipling's famous novel—she was sure the rapture would occur right then and she'd be left behind in the dark palace of sin. Only then did she realize how sheltered she'd been by the warmth and the love and devotion of the deep faith her parents carried and had nurtured in her.

She never quit the faith, never went off somewhere as if angry at what she'd been taught. If Karen Lauber Schell was a rebel, the causes were never faith-shattering. Some of her most precious childhood memories, after all, occurred when she'd come to Nana with a book, climbed up in her ample lap, and listened to stories read by a woman who was always remembered for her smile. Because her mother was working at the store a great deal and her father was mostly traveling as a result of his BIA job, as a child Karen thought of Nana as her mom. As a teenager, that love didn't falter. As a college student, she still considered missions as a profession. As a young professional, she never stopped attending church, never considered abandoning the faith.

She met Paul Schell when she worked in a medical practice in Flagstaff. They dated for just a few months before she was called home because of Nana's precarious health. Paul nobly offered to drive her there. When they arrived at the Rehoboth Christian Hospital Clinic and walked into the room, Nana took one look at the man and told him to promise that he'd take care of Karen—which was somewhat embarrassing given that they weren't quite that far along in their relationship.

It's not hard to tell why Karen and her mother chose, several years ago, to bring an endowment gift to the school and give it in the name of Iva H. Lauber, precious "Nana." Although Christianity had had some kind of impact in the family before Iva (Clara was a Catholic before Mrs. Lauber's mission changed her mother's life), the woman everyone called "Nana" occupies a central position in the pilgrimage of both Clara Chee Lauber and her daughter Karen.

On the Navajo reservation and other reservations, there are times when Christians are ridiculed for aligning themselves with what some more traditional folks believe is the white man's religion. Not long ago, Karen was featured in *Citizen* magazine, a publication of Focus on the Family, for her unflinching opposition to gambling on the reservation. Some Native people see Christianity as being at odds with culture and tradition—and to a certain extent it is.

But it would be difficult to find people more respectful of heritage and clan than Clara Lauber and Karen Schell. Their speech moves easily from Navajo to English. Both of them worked hard to make sure Clara's grandchildren knew how to weave, a longtime family tradition and profession. There are always sheep out back, and Clara and her family still do their own butchering. Every day in the store, the family deals with local Native artists who come to them because their work and worth are respected at Chee's Indian Store.

It would be difficult to find folks more dedicated to the Navajo Nation than Clara

Lauber and Karen Schell. They are women of conviction and integrity—and faith.

Eva Chee

Both Karen and her mother treasure another family story, however, one that is as good as any in describing the two of them. Clara's mother, Eva Chee (her Navajo name is *Eda Bááh Yázhî*), a weaver herself, ran the store long before I-40 came through the reservation. Eva Chee was a member of Tegawitha Catholic Church, just three or four miles east of the interchange where Chee's Indian Store stands today. Clara was baptized there—in fact, her name was changed at the Catholic school, when one of the teachers couldn't pronounce "*a' báhe*" and simply announced that her name would be Clara, after St. Clare.

Her grandparents are buried just down the hill, a few yards from the old stone church that still stands there like a mighty fortress. They'd given the church the land, just a short walk south of their hogan. Clara remembers mass and school and confirmation. She and her family were beloved members of Tegawitha Church, in part because the priests were so thankful for the gift of land.

But one day a Navajo man came around. He was an interpreter for Iva Lauber. He sat with Clara's mother and started to read the Bible from the very beginning, something that the priests had never really done.

That reading was, in fact, a revelation. Clara doesn't know exactly where this happened, because sheep camps were mobile in those days; it could have been anywhere, literally, within miles. But she knows exactly *what* happened.

"My grandma was smart," Karen says; "she wasn't educated, but she was smart." And she was. Her father was an important man, a medicine man, and she used to help him with herbal remedies. "If she'd been educated, we used to say she would have been a lawyer," Clara says.

When the Navajo interpreter got to the story of the flood, Eva Chee listened very closely because she heard something in that story that harmonized with things she'd thought and felt as she'd walked with deliberate care through the beautiful natural world around her. Grandma Chee told Clara that when she used to walk through the brush and grass of the pastureland, she was so filled with wonder that she couldn't help but ask herself who on earth—or elsewhere—could have made all of this beauty.

The man who brought her the Word started to answer that question in a new way, an exciting way, a way the Catholic priests had never tried. Then he came to the story of the flood, and Eva became a whole new

Karen Schell washing windows

kind of believer. She'd found shells herself out there, miles from any ocean. Walking by herself, following the sheep, leading them, she'd come upon evidence for some strange events that even the creation stories of her people didn't fully answer. "Who made all of this?" she kept asking herself.

What she'd heard from the Bible gave her something of an answer to questions she'd asked since she was old enough to wonder. Confidently, she went to the priest and told him that she was fully capable of hearing the Word of God herself, and that what she'd heard from the man who'd read her the Bible had led her to believe that her place was no longer in the Roman Catholic church that was built on what had been her own father's land.

Not long after that she was baptized again in Nana Lauber's mission church, just east of the old Catholic church where her own in-laws were buried. Like the Navajo matriarch she was, she took her whole family with her, including her daughter Clara.

Strength of Character and Conviction

Karen says that when her husband, Paul, decided to return to the reservation, that decision showed his deep love for her. But their daughter, Lisa—a daughter of Paul's from a previous marriage—was not well suited for a school like Sanders, and one of Karen's old teachers told her as much. "You should find another place for her," that woman said. The "other place" was Rehoboth.

But forty miles is still a long way for a bus to go. Karen started a campaign within the Christian churches in the larger community, then asked Gord Kamps, Rehoboth's superintendent, to come and talk to them. Enough people had committed, and the bus was scheduled. Paul and Karen's daughter was in at Rehoboth.

Eighty years earlier, a fifteen-year-old Navajo kid had been cured at the Rehoboth mission hospital. He could speak no English, but quickly enough he told people that the medicine there was better than anything he'd seen. Five generations later, Iva Lauber's grandkids—every one of them who lived in the neighborhood—are enrolled at Rehoboth school on the land where that hospital used to stand. It's quite a story really, but there would have been none at all without the grace of the Lord and the steady dedication of some determined Christian women.

Praise the Lord.

CHAPTER 12

In the Family of God

Herbert F. White

In 1946, Herbert F. White, just 15 years old, got fed up with things at Rehoboth Mission School. He'd gotten himself in trouble more times than he could count, he says; but he was a boy who was becoming a man, and that transition isn't easy for anyone. He'd come to think that the powers that were at Rehoboth were getting far too strict, so just after Thanksgiving break he ran away, literally, and went back home. Running was something he'd always enjoyed, he said, ever since he'd been chasing down horses at home with his father.

Home, for him, was the Pinedale settlement. There, up above the Red Rocks, about twenty miles from Rehoboth, he and his father, Frank White, lived alone. His mother had died soon after he was born. After her death, little Herb was shipped out to Auntie Jennie Hood, "a really sweet lady," he says, who raised him until he began to attend Rehoboth Mission School.

After he left Rehoboth he worked for the railroad but never really left the region. He started out in the kitchen, but eventually worked on the tracks themselves—and

Herbert and Sarah White

that was a promotion. He liked the job and would have stayed there if it hadn't been for his Auntie Jennie, who told him he'd never amount to anything if he didn't get back in school. Auntie Jennie told his father the same thing, and his father insisted.

So the next year Herbert White enrolled at Fort Wingate boarding school, where all

125

Herbert White, football player

that running really got him somewhere. He played every sport possible, including football, where he says he was the fastest guy on the team—so fast that, even as a freshman, he vaulted up to the varsity team where he played for four years. He still has trophies to prove it: Herb White was a runner.

Rehoboth Memories

Even though he had left Rehoboth, even though he'd run away, there were moments at the school that he never forgot, no matter how far he ran. He remembered the sound of the milkman, those milk bottles clanging in the baskets he brought by every morning. Before Rehoboth, Herb had never had fresh cow's milk—goat's milk, sure, but there's a difference, he says.

And there's more he's never forgotten about his Rehoboth days, like the dark night when some of the boys insisted that they'd seen a strange light above the cemetery, an eerie light that seemed to be rushing toward the old dormitory where he and the others were living. Hearing that, he pulled the sheet over his head in his little bed. "It was spooky," he says, as though the whole incident had happened just last week. He was just a kid, too scared to open his eyes.

What he never, ever forgot was the way "Miss Van," a dormitory matron named Marie Vander Weide, came over that night, sat beside him on the bed, and listened to him repeat the story about that spooky light. "No, no, no," she told him, reassuringly, in the Navajo language, her hand on his forehead. "Don't you ever think that way." It was nothing to worry about, she told him, nothing at all. He slept well after that. "She treated me just like a mom," he says today.

Another time he was spooked, probably by a bad dream. Something was coming toward him in the shape of a "v," he remembers, and he started screaming. Miss Van came over. "Honey," she asked, "Herb, what's wrong?" Just like a mother, he says today, so loving. "She hugged me and she started praying for me and it put me back to sleep. I remember that." Just like the mom he never knew.

There's much more to the life of Herb White, of course, but those boyhood memories of sweet comfort never left him. "After I became a born-again Christian," he says, "then I knew what it was that night—it was the love of God, the powerful Spirit himself, the Holy Spirit right there." He can't help but smile when he tells the story. "That's how real it was then—and it is still is now."

But no other single staff member stands as highly—even today—in the memory of Herbert F. White as the woman he knew as Miss Rus. Aletta Rus, a nurse at the hospital,

126

Marie VanderWeide, Rehoboth dormitory "matron," with Rehoboth students at Christmas time

loved and comforted him and even took it upon herself to pay his tuition. Why would she do that? He's not sure, even today. The only reason he can think of is the woman's selfless love. But to explain why she may have paid Herb's tuition requires a broader sense of family and history, something he can only now begin to piece together.

What Herb White remembers, way back when, is a white man, the Rev. Jacob Kamps, coming to the hogan and talking with his father, telling him that Herb should really be going to school. "He kept coming and talking to my dad," he says. He remembers being a little embarrassed when the white man preacher suddenly walked in one day when Herb was dirty, full of flour marks from mixing dough. Rev. Kamps knew a little Navajo and his father knew a little English, "just enough to get along," Herb says.

After a few visits, his father consented to sending Herb to Rehoboth. "That's all right with me," he told the preacher finally, and soon the three of them went off to Rehoboth together.

Why was that decision so easy for Herb's father, a medicine man tied deeply to traditional Navajo ways?

What Herb didn't know then was that a number of his aunts had sent their children to Rehoboth long before. Aunt Jenny Hood, Aunt Ellis Arnold, and Aunt Velma Hodnok—they had all sent their children to Rehoboth.

And there were other connections to Rehoboth too. In those early years, there were few other non-Native health services in the region than those offered at the Rehoboth Christian Hospital. Regularly, the sick and dying would be brought to the hospital.

Aletta Rus (left), nurse at Rehoboth Hospital

Dead bodies held a deep and abiding fear among the Native people, a fear that turned the hospital into something of a repository for those whose health was failing.

Herbert White knows that his father's sister, Hilda White, is buried in the Rehoboth Cemetery. She probably died in the hospital. And today, he thinks, his own father may have sought treatment there, even before Rev. Kamps came to visit the hogan. Perhaps even his mother is buried there, though no one in his family knows for sure. What Herb does know is that even then, in 1940, Rehoboth Mission had played a significant role in his family's life.

In other words, when his father listened to Rev. Kamps assert that his boy, his only child, should go to school at Rehoboth, Herb White believes he assented because his own immediate family had already felt the love and care of people at that mission east of Gallup. He may well have assented because, as early as 1940, the Rehoboth staff had already cared for his extended family in a number of compassionate ways.

Miss Aletta Rus, the woman who picked up the bill for little Herbert's tuition, likely knew several of those family members, and may even have known his own mother.

All those links were part of his father's decision to let his only son, his only child, go off to that boarding school they called Rehoboth. And all of those links help Herb understand why Miss Rus would choose him, as has the Lord God Almighty.

Korea

But there's still more to the story. There's Korea, for example, where one night Herb was on guard duty, "boondocking," he calls it. He was walking around late at night, his rifle loaded, when he heard a whistle, like a gunshot, just over his head. "I looked around, and I was scared—so scared," he says. But just like that John 3:16 popped into his mind, the passage he'd learned to recite at Rehoboth: "For God so loved the world." He'd learned that even in a crisis there was a foundation, a base, a platform from which he could find peace. That Scripture jumped into his mind by way of Rehoboth.

When he was an ornery kid of 15, he ran away from Rehoboth just after Thanksgiving, but what would never leave him, he says, is a foundation he learned—almost without realizing it—for all of life: a belief in God's eternal grace.

When Herb returned from Korea—directly off the ship, in fact—he didn't go back to New Mexico. He went instead to Lawton, Oklahoma, where there was a girl he wanted to see. Sarah Taliman, a girl he remembered fondly from Fort Wingate, was in nursing school there. He'd called her from San Francisco when he and the other GIs stepped off the boat, and she'd been surprised to hear from him that way—surprised, but happy.

A day later he arrived in Lawton, wearing his uniform, his ribbons, and everything. "Is that you?" Sarah asked him. "That's me," he said. Within a year, they were married.

Fifteen years and five children later, Herb was suddenly taken sick. He was drinking too much. The doctor told him he had an ulcer the size of a half-dollar in his stomach and that, if left untreated, it could turn into cancer. So no booze, no steak, no fry bread—just macaroni and cheese—that was the treatment. He'd been living a hard life, working for El Paso Gas at Navajo Station, Arizona, but spending a lot of time riding bulls at rodeos throughout the region, riding and drinking.

In their search for a cure, he and Sarah ended up in Hopi land, where Sarah's mother told them that powerful Hopi medicine men could help him. They found a man with an amazing reputation for healing. He told Herb that the only way to get rid of the ulcer was for it to be sucked out. So the man leaned over and performed the ritual, spitting out what he said was the infected tissue.

Herb White didn't believe it. "'You're a liar,'" he says he told himself. "I thought right then and there that what he showed me was something like paint chips, little white stuff," and he was right. The next day his insides still bothered him, "just like a needle in the stomach."

Things got no better until Sarah saw a sign that said "revival" in Lower Greasewood, where a pastor named Tom White was preaching in the local chapter house. Sarah had been born and reared a Roman Catholic and claims she had no idea what "revival" meant, so she went. But something happened that she couldn't understand. "Something started coming into me," she says. "I felt like I was going to fall or something. Whatever it was they were singing was moving me, but I got scared and left."

She returned to the revival the next night, but left once again, scared about what it was she was feeling in her heart and soul. This time she told her husband that whatever it was they were preaching at that revival was very, very powerful. "You should go," she told him. "You should."

When he did, the preacher stopped him. "What's your need, brother?" he asked him. "God knows your needs." And then he touched him, and right then and there, Herb White fell over and lay on the floor for fifteen minutes. When he got up, tears were running down his cheeks even though he was laughing.

Both Herb and Sarah—and their daughter Frieda—were saved at that revival, and they've been believers—strong and dedicated Christians—ever since. It was September, 1970, thirty years after Herb White's father had gotten into the car with Rev. Jacob Kamps and brought his little boy to Rehoboth Mission School.

In the Family of God

Today, all five kids and Mom and Dad are believers, "and we thank the Lord for that," Sarah says. All of the children attended Rehoboth, two of them graduating. Frieda graduated from Calvin College, and son Fred is serving on the Rehoboth Christian School board and on the Rehoboth National Advisory Council.

And what does Herb White think about those years he spent so long ago at Rehoboth? "All those people back then," he says, remembering Miss Van and Miss Rus and a host of others, "they were humble persons, and the love of Christ was working through them. Rehoboth was really foundational for me—good people, good qualified teachers, a place a child should go to school."

Today his vision expands across the whole reservation. "I pray that we have more of this same type of school—even a college and university so the Navajo Nation can bring itself up and grow in every way because good quality education in love is what the reservation needs."

Herb remembers a time in 1951 when the undefeated Fort Wingate High School football team faced it greatest rival, Gallup High. The stands were full that day, he says, just to see whether little Fort Wingate could knock off the giant. They didn't. The game went into a tie. Herbert White, the running back, remembers breaking away at one point in that game, remembers getting out into the defense and being out in the clear on his way to a touchdown. He remembers thinking this was going to be the big one. And then he tripped. He chuckles a bit at the memory, and he claims that Sarah, who was right there in the stands, never lets him forget that moment.

There are no bleachers full of fans around him today, no crowds; but he hasn't tripped like that in 37 years, hasn't fallen away from the foundational faith given to him in the precious blood of the Lamb through the hands of a matron, a nurse, and many others who loved him dearly. He hasn't been running away for a long, long time. All that's left—for him and his wife and kids—is the end zone. And for all of that, they feel in their hearts a great deal of thanksgiving.

Today Herb and Sarah White are at home in Cornfields, Arizona, at home in the love of the Lord.

On the Road with the Rehoboth Choir

RACHAEL KASS

Members of the Rehoboth Choir

When aging teachers get tired, they'll sometimes grab a huge breath and say things like, "Well, at least it keeps you young"—*it* meaning working with kids. Even though this old teacher has "worked with kids" for just about forty years, I'm not always sure that old line holds much water. Not long ago, I felt ancient, withered, shell-shocked—just plain wiped out.

For several days I traveled with Rehoboth's incredible high school choir. One day, the kids and their marvelous leaders performed at three assemblies in two elementary

131

The Rehoboth Choir

schools on the Rosebud Reservation—all before noon. Just watching the choir hold those kids' attention through all the magical musical shenanigans wore me out. And then this: the moment they were done—even before they had had lunch!—one of the kids picked up a basketball and a dozen of them started playing ball in the gym at St. Francis—that's right, shooting hoops.

After four days with those kids, I swear I'm not a minute younger. It took me two full days of total collapse to feel as though the ship of my state had finally righted.

But I loved it.

One night before a concert at a little church in Mission, South Dakota, the pastor told me that the recent deaths of two young people had added to the incredibly high suicide rate among the Rosebud Sioux. The percentage of people who were taking their own lives was higher there than almost anywhere else in the nation.

The concert that night, like all the others, was electric. When it wasn't haunting in its beauty, it exploded in excitement, every last minute perfectly lit by smiles on the Rehoboth kids' faces, smiles as wide as the Dakota reservation sky.

When it was over, the pastor, who's been preaching at that church for a decade, couldn't stop praising the Lord for the testimony he'd just heard. He told the Rehoboth kids he wasn't sure whether they really understood what they'd done with all that joy they created, what their joy might mean to the kids listening that night, and the hundreds they would be singing for the next day. That pastor just couldn't stop praising the Lord with a chorus of amens and an echoing roll of triumphant hallelujahs.

I'm not Lakota and I'm not from the Rosebud, so I won't even try to speak for the audiences. I'll just speak for me: to hear those kids sing out God's praise like they did put a fire in me. I don't own the adjectives to describe the joy those young people brought to their audiences. I haven't been as thrilled to the core of my soul in a long time as I was by the Rehoboth choir.

After one hundred years, to call Rehoboth Mission—the school, the hospital, the churches—a success isn't particularly difficult. After all, the hospital has become a partner in a first-rate medical facility that serves all the people in the area; the churches still offer God's Word and fellowship in faith; the school is widely recognized as the place where kids get a great education, arguably the best in the whole region.

But let me offer another way of defining success. The choir's own wonderful diversity creates open doors where other schools could likely never enter, and some of those doors open to some of the most troubling social problems of our day. With the Rehoboth choir, I traveled into places I likely wouldn't have gone without them, and I was blessed to be privy to the witness they bring to people whose lives perhaps too often seem bereft of joy. I saw them witness to God's love in a musical presentation that throbbed with the joy of several dozen smiling faces, happy to be there, happy to bring love wherever they went.

Some people say that in our postdoctrinal age—at a time when people are perhaps more "spiritual" than they've been, but sometimes not particularly "religious" (there's a difference), a time when folks search for meaning but may not look too diligently in churches—the future of evangelism, of bringing people to the Lord, may well lie, simply, in offering beauty to a yearning world. What may bring people to

JOHN VAN'T LAND

133

belief in God Almighty may not be reason or truth or even well-honed doctrine, but the brilliance of a rainbow in a grey world.

By way of music and stories and sheer fun, the Rehoboth kids spread beauty wherever they went. A rainbow is what I saw in that church in Mission, South Dakota, and in every school where those kids sang. A rainbow—beauty from the Lord.

Hallelujah, that Lakota pastor said, over and over again.

Yeah, this old man said, trying to get his breath. Amen and amen.